TRADITIONAL JU-JITSU GROUNDWORK

NEWAZA

WRITTEN BY SIMON PALMER

SENTOU SERIES
VOLUME 1

68 ARM LOCKS/WRIST LOCKS
50 CHOKES, STRANGLES AND NECK CRANKS
25 HOLD DOWNS/PINS
19 LEG/ANKLE LOCKS
OVER 470 COLOUR PHOTOS.

Traditional Ju Jitsu Groundwork : Newaza
Sentou Series : Volume 1

Copyright © Simon Palmer 2017 All Rights Reserved
The rights of Simon Palmer to be identified as the author of this work have been asserted in accordance with the Copyright, Designs and Patents Act 1988
All rights reserved. No part may be reproduced, adapted, stored in a retrieval system or transmitted by any means, electronic, mechanical, photocopying, or otherwise without the prior written permission of the author or publisher.

Spiderwize
Remus House
Coltsfoot Drive
Woodston
Peterborough
PE2 9BF

www.spiderwize.com

A CIP catalogue record for this book is available from the British Library.

The views expressed in this work are solely those of the author and do not necessarily reflect the views of the publisher, and the publisher hereby disclaims any responsibility for them.

ISBN: 978-1-911113-97-3

TRADITIONAL JU JITSU GROUNDWORK

NEWAZA

SENTOU SERIES
VOLUME 1

THE ART OF JAPANESE JU JITSU GROUND FIGHTING.

FOREWORD

It will be generally agreed that a manual of this quality should serve a double purpose, for not only is Ju Jitsu to be commended as an excellent form of exercise for adults and youngsters alike in developing all round physical development, but the mastery of even a few of its many holds, throws, strangles and arm locks affords the pupil of either sex a highly effective means of dealing with an attack.

I have never been prone to advance exaggerated claims for the supernormal efficiency of any martial art against an armed and resolute aggressor, but none the less, within my own long experience, both as a pupil and now senior instructor, I firmly believe a Ju Jitsu training manual of this quality, coupled with regular exercise, preferably at a Ju Jitsu club, affords the best possible chance of surviving an attack.

Kevin Pell 9th Dan Hanshi
Founder and Chief Instructor Ishin Ryu Ju Jitsu
National Representative European Ju Jitsu Union

CONTENTS

1) Introduction .... 7 - 8

2) Brief history of Ju Jutsu .... 8 - 9

3) Ju Jutsu, Ju Jitsu, or Jujitsu? 9

5) Hold downs (Osae Komi Waza) 10-29

6) Pins .... 30 - 37

7) Arm locks (Kansetsu Waza) 38-80

8) Wrist locks (Tekubi Waza) 81-96

9) Foot/leg locks (Ashi Waza) 97-109

10) Strangles and chokes (Shime Waza) 110-157

11) Neck locks (Kubi Gatami) 158-164

12) Advanced quick chokes 165-169

13) Turning the opponent over (Uke) 175-179

14) Staying on all fours 180

15) Painful distraction techniques 181

16) Sit ups 182-183

17) About the Author 184

18) Index 185-192

TRADITIONAL JU JITSU GROUNDWORK

Many thanks to the team who helped me. Without you this wouldn't have been possible:

Martin Winchester, Mark Wood, CJ, Andy Honey, Chris Cunningham, Damien Cunningham, Emily Millgate and Nick Fitzpatrick.

WARNING

Techniques shown within this book can be very dangerous and must be done with great care. The author or anybody involved with this book cannot accept responsibility for any injuries caused by copying techniques explained here.

'TORI' AND 'UKE'

The Japanese terms Tori and Uke will be used throughout this book.

Tori: The person doing the technique or attacking.

Uke: The person receiving the technique and being attacked.

WHY WE USE TRADITIONAL JAPANESE TRANSLATION:

We use the Japanese translation firstly out of respect, and secondly because it doesn't matter where in the world we teach or train, if it is a Japanese Martial Art then we can all understand the commands given.

INTRODUCTION

The aim of this book is to relight the passion of Japanese Newaza (groundwork) and bring back to life the techniques used in Japanese Ju Jutsu and Judo.

Jigoro Kano founded Judo in 1882 and although he derived it from Ju Jutsu, Jigoro took out many techniques to create a style that had maximum efficiency with minimum effort. Also, with some of the more dangerous techniques taken out, Judo was more appealing to a wider audience. Thus, Judo became a sport and a very good sport at that: in 1964 it was introduced into the Olympics in Tokyo and every year since 1972 Judo has been a significant Olympic spectacle. For some reason, many traditional Ju Jutsu clubs these days tend to favour the stand-up side and focus on strikes, locks, strangles and throws (though there are some great clubs out there that still practise both stand-up and groundwork). However, there are no rules in Japanese Ju Jutsu groundwork, so as a martial art it becomes a lot more fun, it enhances the senses – and it develops reactions and sheer bloody mindedness. Unfortunately, when martial arts are mentioned today most non-martial artists think of Kick-boxing, Brazilian Ju Jitsu or MMA (mixed martial arts). All these are rules-based sports and stick to safer techniques prescribed by their rules. Japanese Ju Jutsu, meanwhile, has no rules and because I visit other clubs to cross-train, it results in me getting told off for using illegal moves! It seems health and safety has gone mad and common sense has gone altogether.

I have practised many different martial arts over extensive years and can discern which techniques work better than others. I have researched hundreds of techniques and I believe that the ones in this book work best. I have seen some awful techniques, some great ones and some that are too flashy to be useful in reality. Some of these techniques you will know, some you won't, and some will probably be demonstrated differently from what you have learnt with other people – but I aim mainly to teach you how easy it is to finish a fight, on the ground.

These are all basic Ju Jitsu techniques, no counters or escapes.

Make sure you warm up your whole body to prevent any injuries and run through the techniques slowly to begin with before getting more vigorous.

When these techniques are being applied, if you feel any discomfort or pain, tap your partner or the mat nice and hard. As the Uke (person being attacked), 'tap out' immediately if you feel the move is 'on'. DO NOT WAIT, especially with chokes and strangles, which cut off oxygen or blood to the brain. With a lock, a screaming Uke normally means it's too late and some part of the Uke's body isn't where it should be. With chokes and strangles, the Tori (attacker) must note that no scream or tap from the Uke may mean the Uke has lost consciousness...

...Seriously, **BE CAREFUL!**

A VERY BRIEF HISTORY

Although modern Ju Jutsu is practised more as a self-defence art to overcome an opponent with minimal effort, traditionally it was used in kill-or-be-killed situations, therefore it focused on literally annihilating the attacker. The purpose of many techniques would have been to snap, crack, pop or break something. Some techniques were just about killing.

Ju Jutsu was founded by Takenouchi Hisamori during the Senjoky period of the Muromachi period in 1532. Takenouchi created a system that could be used on a battlefield in which an unarmed warrior could defeat another warrior who was armed or unarmed. The use of strikes was pointless because punching or kicking armour would just be daft! For the same principle ground fighting wasn't really used either, because ending up on the ground would probably get you stabbed. And, again, it would be very hard to fight an opponent wearing armour.

Things started to change for Ju Jutsu in the Edo period between 1603-1868 as strict laws were put into place to reduce wars and conflict. The wearing of armour and carrying weapons were made illegal. Hand-to-hand combat evolved with the use of strikes, kicks, grappling and ground fighting. Ground fighting became even more prominent when Kano incorporated it in Kano Ju Jutsu (aka early Judo) after losing bouts against other clubs that trained heavily in Newaza (groundwork).

JU JUTSU, JU JITSU OR JIUJITSU: WHICH IS RIGHT?

In brief, the only correct spelling is 'Ju Jutsu', which is taken from the official Anglicization of Japanese. All the other spellings started around 100 years ago during a time when the correct pronunciation of Japanese was not widely known. As the system spread so did the name, but it was rarely written down so different spellings propagated due to phonetic mistakes.

Ju Jutsu

Ju = soft, pliable, flexible or gentle.

Jutsu = technique, science or art.

Therefore, Ju Jutsu: the Gentle Art

Judo

Ju = soft, pliable, flexible or gentle

Do = path or way

So, Judo: the Gentle Way.

OSAE KOMI : HOLD DOWNS

Hold downs, or Osae Komi, are vital in groundwork; they let you take control, relax and asses your next move, such as applying an arm lock or a strangle. Hold downs are best used to restrain someone until help comes or they calm down.

A hold down gives you the opportunity to move freely around the body (especially if your opponent is a wriggler!). The key to moving freely is to keep your weight on an opponent at all times, leaving no gaps between you and the opponent's body. The only time you leave gaps is when transitioning from a hold to certain arm or leg locks. Keep relaxed as much as possible, as the more relaxed you are the more freely you will move. Tensing and holding on as tightly as you can will fatigue you really quickly and make it easier for the opponent to escape. A relaxed body is harder to move than a ridged one.

Use elbows, forearms and the head to manipulate an opponent, causing them as much pain as you can to move them where you want them. Elbow points, for example, are used tactically to cause an opponent to turn away from the pain – a fantastic distraction to hinder any counter attack.

After throwing an opponent, fall on top of them with all your body weight and get straight into a hold down. This can wind them and even crack a rib. Koshi Guruma (loin wheel) into Kesa Gatame (scarf hold); Tai Otoshi (body drop) into Kesa Gatame (scarf hold); or Te Guruma (hand wheel) into Yoko Shiho Gatame (side four quarters) – done properly, these can be very strong combinations and end a fight quickly.

The main reason for hold downs is so attackers can't keep on attacking you once they have hit the floor. Get them held down as soon as possible, take control of the situation and then break an arm or leg, or make them pass out (in real life – not in a friendly club situation, obviously). You don't want to roll about on the floor for hours on end getting tired, perhaps for a minute at the very most. Disable them, then get up in case there are more attackers to deal with or escape from.

Which is the best hold depends on the size of your opponent. Trying to get the mount (see top pic) or side four quarters (see bottom pic) on someone who likes their food can be tricky; you will end up see-sawing on top of their belly.

KESA GATAME
SCARF HOLD

Kesa Gatame is a very easy hold and from which many locks, strangles, neck cranks and punching possibilities arise.

Key points are:

1. With this and all holds, keep your weight on the opponent. In scarf hold, or Kesa Gatame, the weight must be on their chest and shoulder.

2. Keep your head pressed to their head so your weight is kept low and the head is also protected from punches and grabs.

3. Keep your legs nice and wide (the 'running legs' in the top picture) to help with stability.

4. When your opponent tries to escape stay relaxed and just swizzle around with them, maintaining the 'running-legs, head-pressed' position. Don't panic or tense up too much.

5. Hold onto the opponent's arm that is in front of you. Hold it just above the elbow, pinning it in tightly to your waist to stop it flailing out (see middle picture).

6. If your opponent is stronger than you, you could modify the scarf hold to a 'pillow hold' (bottom pic): Bring your lead running knee up to the opponent's head; grab the Gi of this leg using the hand of the arm wrapped around their neck, forming a 'noose' around their neck. This is a strong hold as it puts more pressure on their neck and makes opponents tire quickly. You've a good chance of getting a tap, even from a strong guy.

KAMI SHIHO GATAME
UPPER FOUR QUARTERS HOLD

Kami shiho Gatame is a tight hold and can make it extremely hard for an opponent to breath. It is easy to change from Kesa Gatami to this hold. This hold is ideal for kneeing your opponent on the head, striking the floating ribs with fists and elbows, or give a hammer fist/open hand strike to the groin.

Points to remember are:

1. To keep elbows up high under your opponent's armpits (see top pic). This will make it very hard for them to punch you or use their arms to escape.
2. Keep legs out wide for stability, never together.
3. Keep your head down and your weight on their chest (see middle pic).
4. You can have your opponent's arms outside or tucked in under your own.
5. Hold on to opponent's belt or Gi bottoms (trousers)

USHIRO KESA GATAME
REVERSE SCARF HOLD

This hold is a very good transition from upper four quarters and it also lets you have a great view and feel of their arm and legs.

Striking points are the ribs and groin, but it is also a great position from which to get a neck crank on (see page 160)

Points to remember are:

1. Hold opponent's elbow, same as in Kesa Gatame, just below the elbow and pinned into your waist (see top pic).
2. Keep your other elbow (not seen in this pic) high into their armpit to keep Uke's arm out of the way and wedge your hand in their side.
3. Put weight on Uke's chest and shoulder.
4. Push with your feet to put more pressure on Uke's chest, push down and across.
5. It is a good idea to trap their other arm between your arm and their body.

HOLD DOWNS

USHRIO KESA GATAME (REVERSE SCARF HOLD

CLOSE UP OF HOLDING ARM

As you can see, there is plenty of opportunity and room to strike the ribs and still have control of the arm.

17

YOKO SHIHO GATAME
SIDE FOUR QUARTERS HOLD

This is a very popular and strong hold with a different ways of applying it.

The most common locks from here are Ude Gatame (figure four/entangled lock. Also, see page 54) and Ushiro Ude Gatame (reverse figure four) but don't forget there are plenty of other locks and strangles to do and many striking points.

Points to remember are:

1. Put weight on Uke's chest with elbows tucked in (see top pic).

2. If possible trap your opponent's arms, one pinned next to your body and the other pinned with your elbow next to their body (see bottom pic).

3. Keep watch of Uke's legs, so you can see what they are trying to do.

4. If you haven't got Uke's arm, then make sure your cover your head so it can't be hit (top pic)

HOLD DOWNS

YOKO SHIHO GATAME (SIDE FOUR QUARTERS)

DIFFERENT WAYS OF APPLYING YOKO SHIHO GATAME

1. Elbows wedged into the side of the Uke, one tight under the armpit, the other in their hip (fig 1).
2. Trapping Uke's arm against their body (fig 2).
3. With one arm around Uke's neck and the other between their legs (fig 3).
4. With the arm under the Uke's body grab their wrist and pull it in tight. This immobilises the top half of their body completely (fig 4).
5. With your arm under Uke's head grab the top of their arm close to the shoulder (fig 5).

STRIKING AND KNEEING FROM YOKO SHIHO GATAMI

The striking points are numerous from this hold, from the face all the way down to the thighs (fig 5).

Elbows to the head, ribs and thighs (fig 1 and 2).

Knees to the head and ribs (fig 6 and 7).

Forearm across the face (fig 8).

TATE SHIHO GATAME
BODY CROSS HOLD

Possibly this is the most dominating hold-down with many options for locks, strangles and strikes. There are many ways to make your opponent surrender – for example, fingers in the eyes, pinching their top lip, or placing your thumb in the underside of their jaw line (fig 5).

In fig 1, the Uke has an arm around your waist, but in fig 2, I have got under the Uke's arms and wrapped them around his head.

Points to remember are:

1. Don't come up too high on your knees – keep all of your weight down on the Uke.
2. As the Uke tries to escape, act like a lizard on hot sand by extending your arms and legs out in the same direction the Uke tries to roll you in. This makes it hard to be rolled (fig 3).
3. Take control of the Uke's arms with your legs to unleash strikes (fig 4).
4. Don't lay up too high on your opponent – stay with your knees either side of the Uke's waist area.
5. Push the Uke's arm out ready for the next hold-down (fig 6).

TATE SHIHO GATAME (BODY CROSS)

FIG 1

FIG 2

FIG 3 ARM OUT TO STABILIZE

FIG 4 CONTROLLING THE ARMS

FIG 5 THUMB UNDER JAW LINE

FIG 6 GETTING THE ARM READY

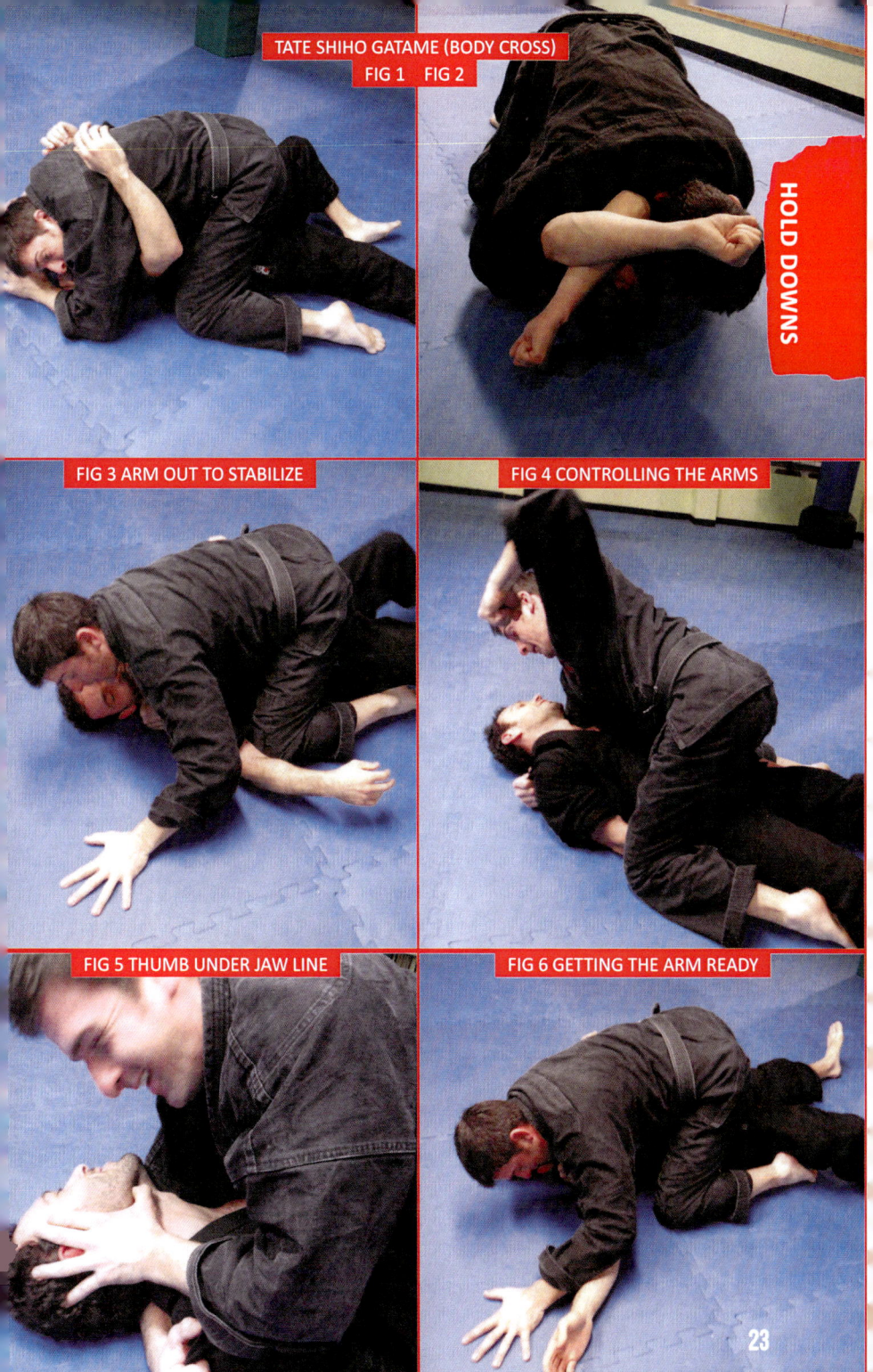

KATA GATAME
SHOULDER HOLD

It is easy to transition from the Tate shiho Gatame (Body cross) into this very strong, tight hold, with the added extra of a strangle. This hold is extremely hard to get out of and uses little energy. You can stick your leg out to stabilize yourself if the Uke is trying to roll you over. The leg also aids as a counter weight if the Uke tries to roll away from you – though if they do, the strangle will go on even tighter!

Key points are:

1. Keep your knees up tight and high next to your opponent's shoulder, if possible, to concentrate all of your weight on one small area (fig 1).

2. Make sure that your opponent's arm is bent tight over one side of their neck and face. Push Uke's Tricep with your neck and slightly lean your body towards them to increase weight (fig 2).

3. Use the 'monkey grip' (curled fingers hooked together) to place the strangle (fig 3), or grab your own shoulder/Gi as high up as you can.

HOLD DOWNS

KATA GATAME (SHOULDER HOLD)
FIG 1
FIG 2
FIG 3

SUMMARY: HOLD DOWNS

All the hold downs we have learnt so far can be used with the opponent on their front. A fact that is normally over looked are the opportunities for many strangles and locks. When, as is often the case, you see fighters trying to turn their opponents over onto their back, they are wasting time and energy. It makes sense to hold your opponent facedown before they have time to either attack, turn themselves over on their back, or stand up. If you have their back, you have control.

This also gives you lots of striking points, such as the back of the head, the neck, ribs or spine. With some of these holds, the strangle or lock is already on.

Kesa-Gatame: The strangle is automatically on with this hold and an easy arm lock is possible, too (fig 1).

Kame-Shiho-Gatame: A very frustrating hold for the Uke, whose face is squashed on the mat while you squeeze the breath out of them (fig 2).

Ushiro-Kesa-Gatami: A very easy and effective hold (fig 3).

Yoko-Shiho-Gatami: This is a lovely hold. When you try to bring your hands together, it bends Uke's spine at the same time strangling and compacting the side of their body. It is very uncomfortable for the Uke (fig 4).

Tate-Shiho-Gatami: This is not the strongest of holds (fig 5) as the Uke can push you up quite easily. But as they do, it leads to Hadaka-Jime (Naked strangle, fig 6) with ease .

URA GATAME
REAR HOLD

Ura Gatame is not the most practical of holds. But if you do manage to achieve it, then it can put great strain on the Uke's back and the more you roll forward, the more pressure you put on Uke's neck.

One way of getting into this hold is when the Uke is on all fours and you trap their arm with your legs (see fig 1/2), making sure your legs are crossed. Then bend over and grab their other arm (fig 1).

Now you have two options: the safe way, and the not-so-safe way. The safe way is to pull the Uke's arm up and sit back down so that they are forced to roll over and lay on your chest.

The not-so safe-way is to do a forward roll and pull their arm back with your legs.

Once the Uke is on top of you (fig 3), twist your body towards their head so that their hips are wedged upwards and their weight is transferred on to their neck (fig 4).

From this position you now have a choice of striking or going for a strangle or arm lock.

FIG 1 BEND OVER TO GRAB UKE'S ARM

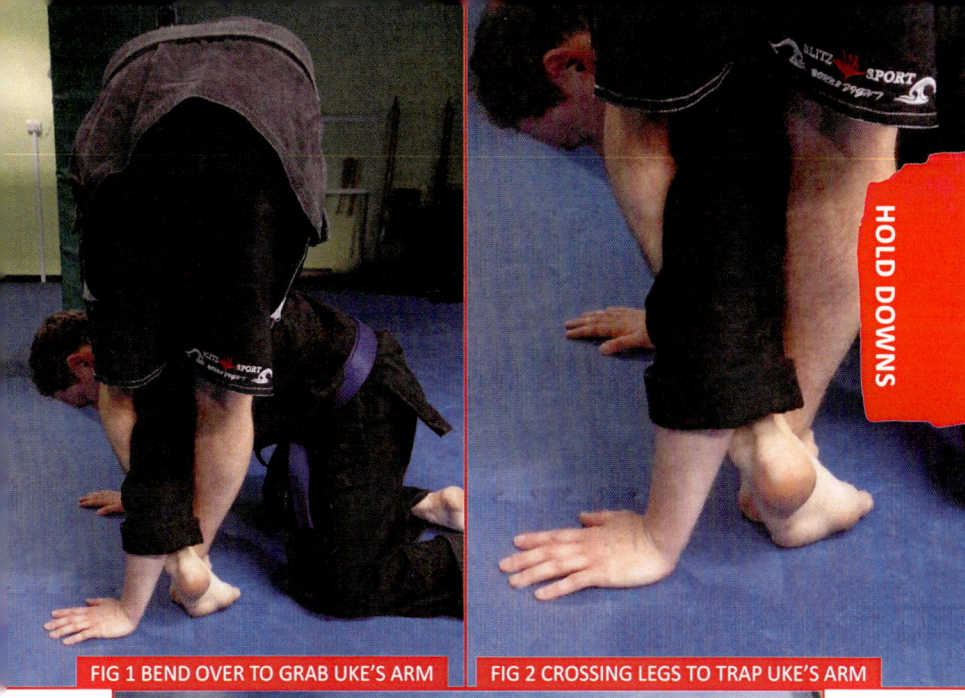

FIG 2 CROSSING LEGS TO TRAP UKE'S ARM

HOLD DOWNS

FIG 3

FIG 4

29

PINS

Pins are slightly different to hold-downs in that you are not on the floor with your opponent; instead you are kneeling or standing next to them.

If you have an injury (or are wearing your best suit!), you don't want to be rolling about on the floor. You want to just pin an attacker down and wait for help.

Pins are great for inflicting pain and allowing you all-round visual awareness. Seeing that more trouble is approaching, you can disable your opponent quickly (SNAP!) and still have a good chance of dealing with people silly enough to try their luck.

The next eight pins should all flow one from the other, helping you to remember and apply them when needed.

TRICEP PIN

The first pin I will take you through is so easy, so very effective you won't believe it will work. It is great for gaining all-round visual awareness.

Once the Uke is on their front, place your shin on to their Tricep.

Keeping the top of your foot on the ground, place a great deal of weight on to the Tricep. You can be either side of the arm but remember to have a good solid base so you can't be taken off balance; you can put your hand on the Uke's back to support yourself and keep them from moving.

PINS

KNEELING SHOULDER PIN

From the Tricep pin, you can grab the Uke's wrist, lever it straight upwards while taking your knee off the Uke's Tricep and turning to face the Uke. Get your knees close into their head and rib cage, and rest their hand/wrist on your shoulder. Place both hands on to their shoulder and pull it in towards your body. Remember to keep your back straight. If you move your hands up to their elbow you can apply the arm crush or straight-arm lock.

Again with this technique there are many striking points, such as knife-hand strikes to the neck, knees to the head, or a hammer fist to the back and ribs.

STRAIGHT-ARM LOCK PIN

From the kneeling shoulder pin, grab the Uke's wrist. If you are grabbing with your left hand (see pic) then place your forearm on your left thigh and bring your right knee up, slipping it over the Uke's elbow. You need to make sure that your left arm is locked and strong because the pressure from the knee pushing down on the Uke's elbow will be very strong. Also make sure that you have good balance and are able to look around easily.

In the picture, though it is hard to see, my right foot is on the ground and touching the Uke's body for extra stability. My right hand is free so I can strike to the Uke's head or – if my opponent is strong and I need more strength – I can hold the Uke's wrist with both hands.

PINS

BENT-ARM PIN
"POLICEMAN'S PIN"

Remember that these moves flow from one to the other, so from the straight-arm pin bend the Uke's left arm towards you whilst sliding your right knee from the Tricep over on to their body. Keep twisting their arm until it is tight up their back. You will get more leverage if you keep hold of their wrist; the higher the Uke's wrist goes up their back, the more pain they'll feel.

In the picture I have the Uke's wrist a bit lower so that I can get my left hand tight under their arm. I am grabbing the Uke's Gi, and as I move my forearm up this applies a shoulder lock.

From this position it is easy to grab Uke's other arm so that you have both arms behind their back. If the Uke is flexible and can straighten their arms from there, just lean forward and put your chest on their arms.

STANDING STRAIGHT-ARM PIN

From the single or double bent-arm pin grab the wrist of one arm and straighten the arm as you stand up. Make sure that your feet are wedged in as tight as possible to the Uke's waist. Hold the arm straight up, pushing it slightly towards Uke's other shoulder as this puts pressure/pain into their shoulder (fig1).

One arm is usually enough to stop them going anywhere, but if you want to make sure, grab their other wrist and push the wrists towards each other (fig2).

PINS

FIG 1

FIG 2

To apply an arm lock keep holding on to the Uke's wrists and move them out enough so that you can step over one arm, make sure that the back of your leg is against their arm, keep your leg bent and your heel up, also check that the Uke's palm is facing your leg. When putting the lock on straighten your leg, putting your heel on the floor.

PIN USING BOTH SHINS

This is most commonly used after a throw. Keeping hold of the Uke's wrist, lift their arm and give them a good kick in the back or head (fig 1); this will make sure they are on their side so we know that their bottom hand is trapped under their body. Place one shin on the floating rib and the other across the neck or head. Using your weight to pin your opponent you can apply an arm lock if you needed (fig 2). Again it is very important that you have a good base and don't lean forward, so keep your back straight and posture strong. You should have one hand free to be able to strike the face, ribs or to help break the arm.

If Uke is stronger/quicker than you and they pull their arm away before you lock it, you can always apply the wrist lock. Either fold their arm downwards (fig 1) and hold the back of their hand (preferably by the knuckles). Then apply a figure four wrist lock (fig 2). If you need to pick Uke up then it is easy with this lock, as you can control the amount of pain that goes through the wrist. Tell them to get up as that normally makes it easier because they understand what you are doing.

FIG 1

FIG 2

PINS

But if you feel nasty then just grab the back of their hand with both of your hands and pull straight upwards keeping pressure on their head and ribs with your shins.

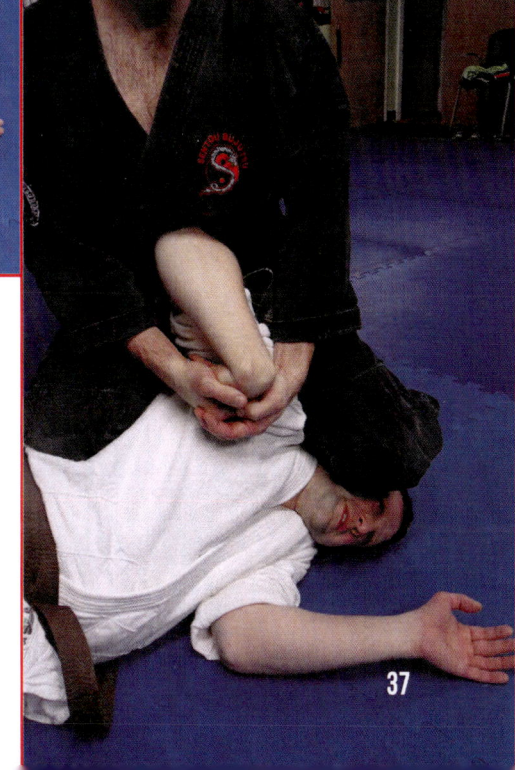

ARM AND WRIST LOCKS
KANSETSU WAZA AND TEKUBI WAZA

Arm and wrist locks are a big part of ground fighting, either to make your opponent comply, or to break them piece by piece. Arm and wrist locks use leverage to work the opponent's wrist, elbow or shoulder. You put great pressure on them with the least effort by hyper flexing, hyper extending or hyper rotating the joints or ball sockets. If you need to put a lot of strength behind a technique then you are usually doing it wrong.

Competition locks are generally safer and take longer to apply so Uke has more time to tap out. You need to maximise your arsenal as much as possible to have a much better chance of winning any fights, so some of these techniques – applied very quickly – are not allowed in competition. Some of them shown here can be used standing as well as on the ground. It is always good to play around and see where these techniques can be used and how effective they are in different positions. Don't get stuck in thinking that there is only one way to apply a lock or strangle; just because you've been shown a technique in one position doesn't mean it's the only way it will work. Straight-arm locks and figure four locks are the most versatile and can be applied from many different positions.

There is a misconception that traditional Japanese standing Ju Jitsu locks are only used standing up. I find traditional Ikkio and Nikio locks, for example, just as effective or possibly more effective and easier to apply when on the ground.

Be 'proud' when putting locks on: head up, chest out and arms strong. If you keep yourself curled up the lock won't go on as well.

ARM & WRIST LOCKS

39

JU JI GATAMI
CROSS ARM LOCK OR ARM BAR

Now we are going to take a look at Ju ji Gatami. There are many ways to apply this lock we have seen four different ways in this book already.

The general rule-of-thumb is hold on to the Uke's wrist and put pressure on the back of the elbow however you can, making sure the arm is locked out straight. This can be achieved in numerous ways.

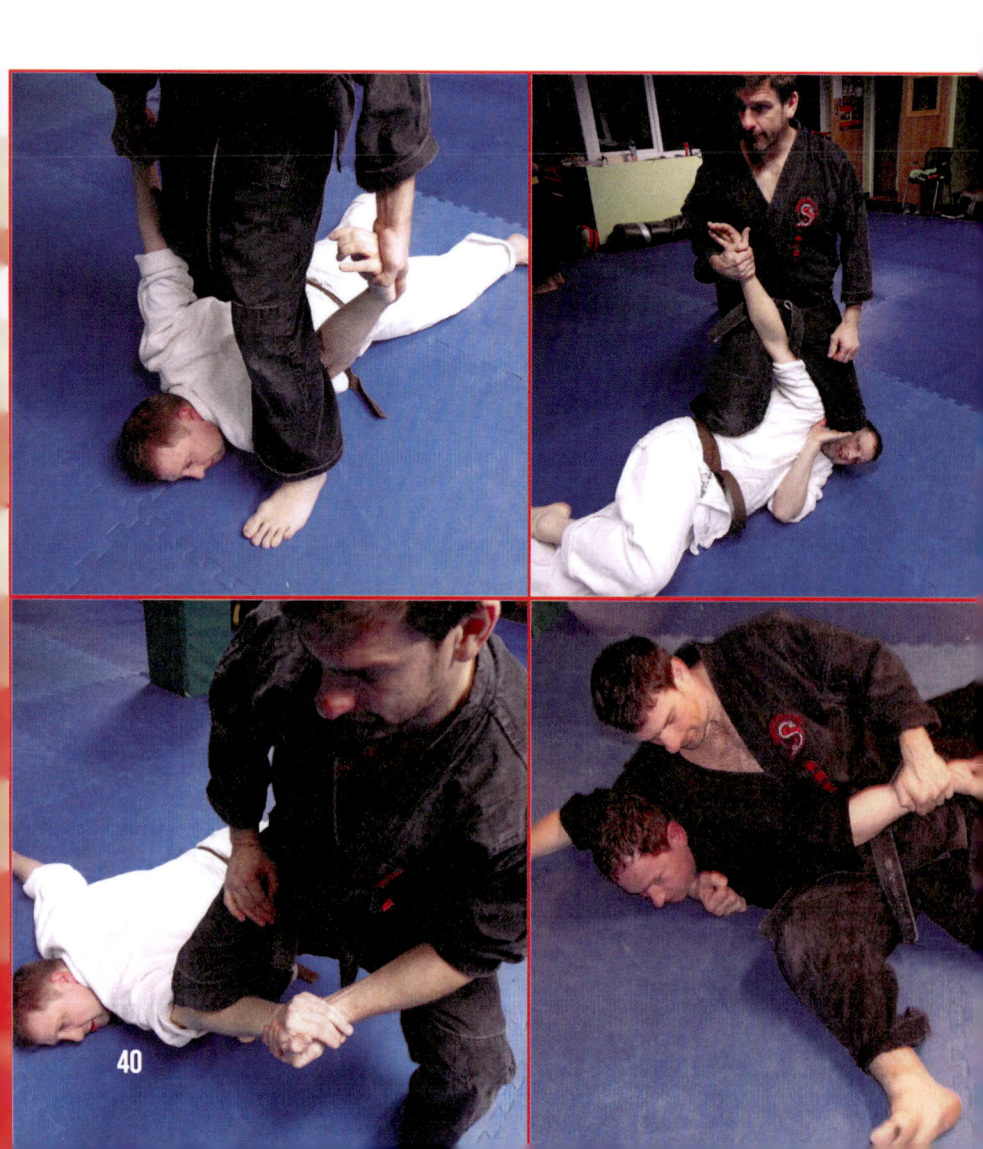

Everybody has seen the first one – but I have a different take on it.

To start with, put your bottom as close to the Uke as possible and keep the Uke's wrist touching your body as you lay back with it.

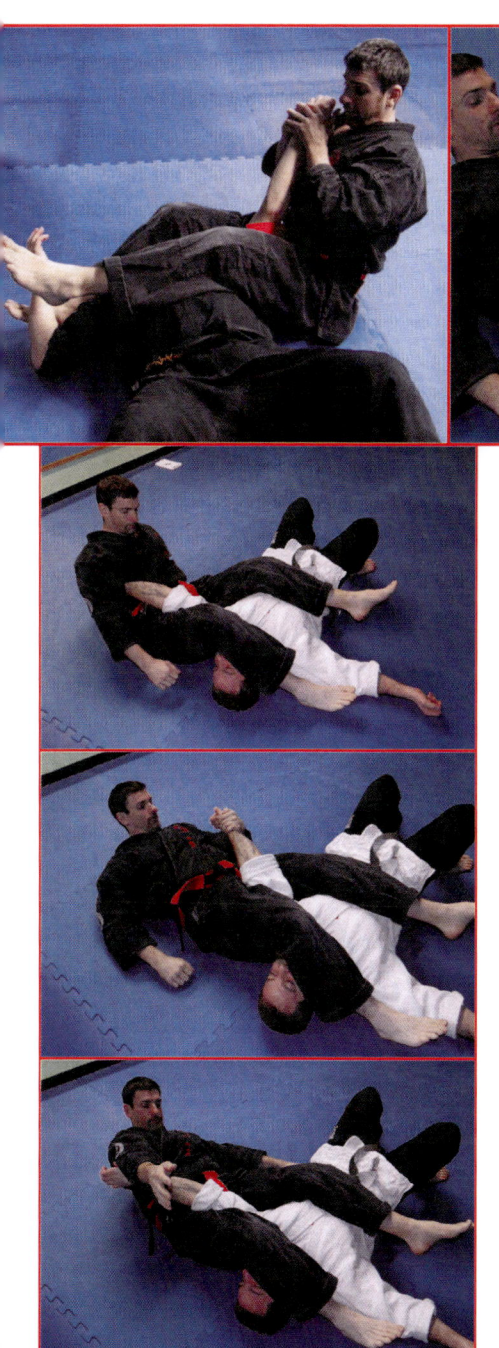

ARM & WRIST LOCKS

Once you are on your back if you are slim enough you can keep Uke's hand in the middle of your chest and lift your hips to apply the lock. But if you have plenty of 'relaxed muscle' you will find it easier to move the Uke's arm to the side of your body and lift your hip up, otherwise the Uke's arm will just lay across your belly and the lock won't work.

You can put the lock on over either hip as long as you make sure that the back of Uke's elbow is against your thigh. It is possible to trap their arm with your armpit or forearm for more leverage.

41

TWISITNG

From the start of the lock the Uke will try to get out of it by twisting and turning before their arm is straightened and locked. So, when you're sitting before laying back and taking control of the arm, you can twist it by the wrist as far round as it will go, trying to keep it straight. This will put stress on and stretch the muscles and ligaments in the arm and shoulder. You will feel their arm tighten and they will tap well before your back touches the mat. The arm can be twisted either way depending on which way Uke twists.

The top two pictures show the arm is twisted one way. The bottom two show the other way, the arm is twisted so far round the hand faces the same way. I grab the wrist with both hands to ensure good leverage. On all four of these pictures the Uke is tapping, which shows how little distance you need to lean back.

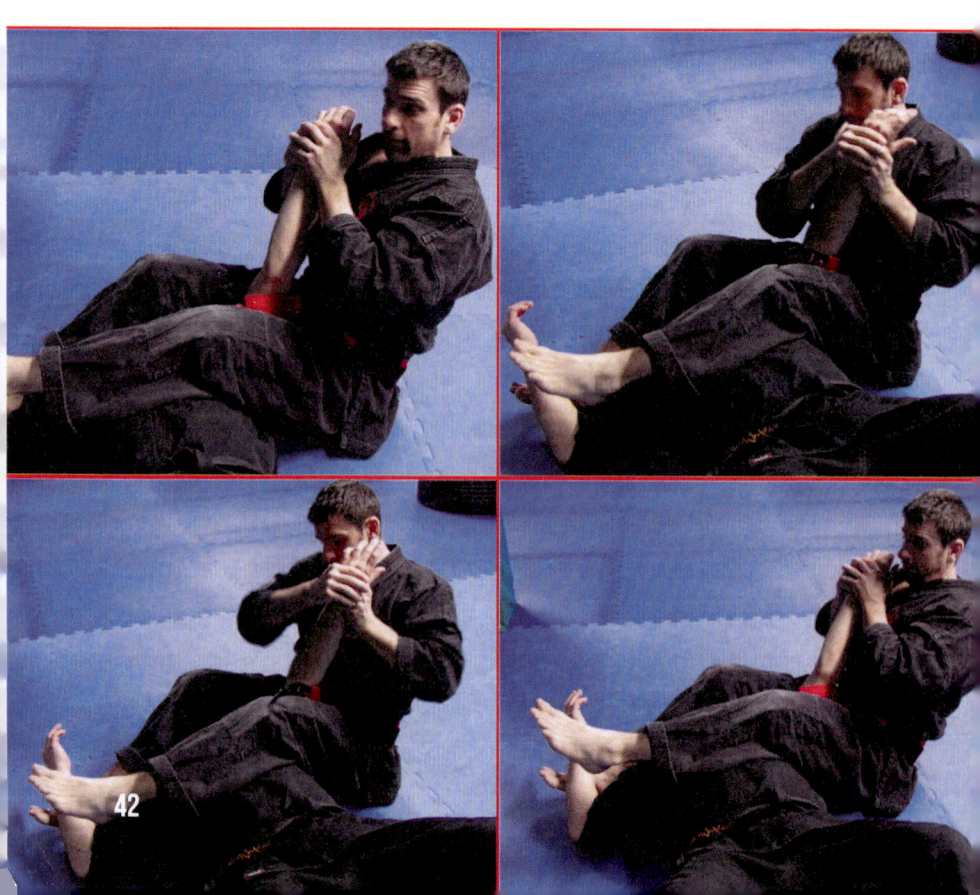

BREAKING THE GRIP

There are a few ways to break the grip if the Uke has gripped both hands together. Place your foot on Uke's furthest arm and pull with all your might, but this wastes energy. Here are some much easier ways. The first way is to locate Uke's thumb and press the top of their thumb into itself. Below left, my hand is the very bottom one. With my index and middle fingers I am squeezing Uke's thumb. Another way could be to pull the thumb straight back (below right)

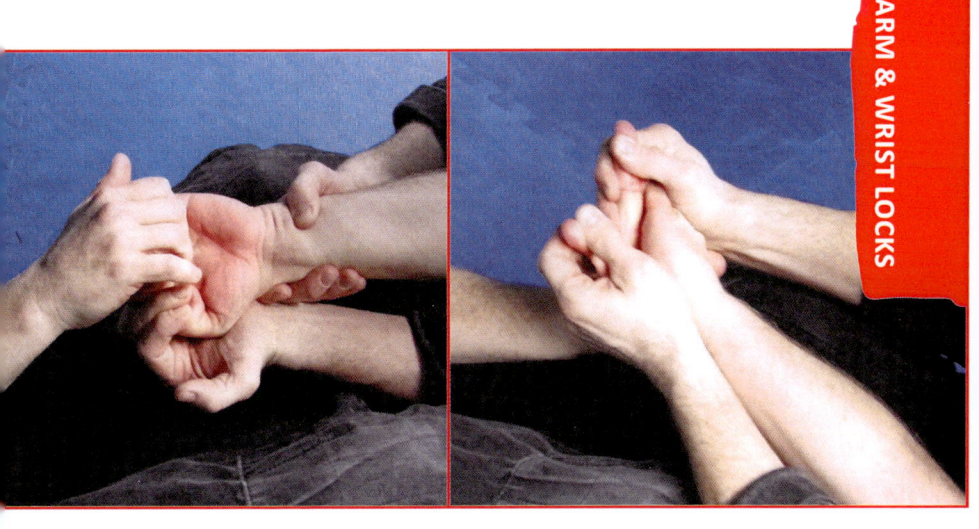

ARM & WRIST LOCKS

Or
ease out the little finger and pull that straight back. If Uke is strong, take the little finger, bend it 90% and then twist: they will let go.

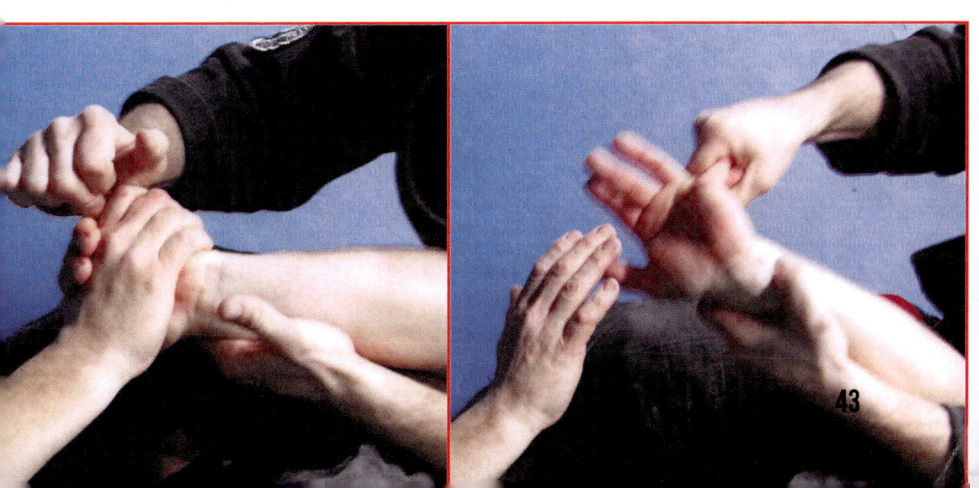

By placing your foot on to the thigh of your other leg (see below) you can apply this lock much quicker, creating more instant pain. Make sure that the Uke's elbow is on or just above your shin and keep your other leg over the Uke's neck. Pull the Uke's arm more towards your knee and this will keep their arm in the direction of their hip, making it harder for them to roll out.

From Kesa-Gatami (scarf hold) this lock is very easy to apply by placing your bottom 'running leg' on or just above the Uke's elbow and clasping your top leg over the arm, pushing down on their wrist (see below). But remember the Uke's other hand is free so be quick before they notice.

The straight-arm lock applied from Yoko-Shiho Gatami (side four quarters) is applied from the figure four hand position (see below) and with the weight on Uke's chest. My left hand is holding Uke's wrist (thumbs on the outside) and my right forearm is lifting up beneath their elbow. This leaves the Uke wide open for knees to the ribs, elbows to the face, neck and ribs. You can also trap their other arm under your knee.

For the same lock but done facing Uke from above, have one hand on their shoulder and the other holding on to your own wrist. Keep the Uke's forearm trapped under your armpit, locked in tight. A slight lift up will stop Uke from punching you with their free hand. Keep your oppsite knee on the ground and the knee up with your foot on the ground to give you more stability and height.

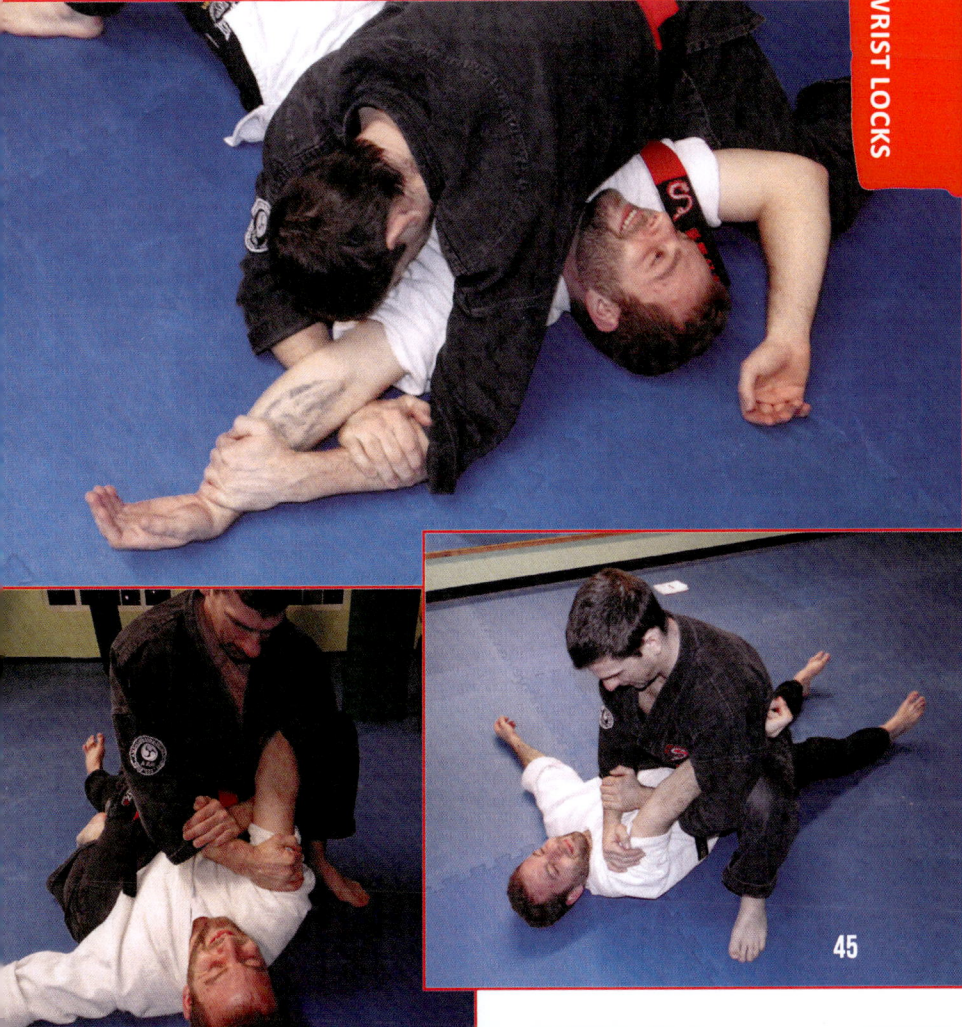

ARM & WRIST LOCKS

The last lock along with the next three locks can be applied standing up as well. With your back against Uke's chest (see below) apply the same figure four technique. Using your forearm under the Uke's elbow and holding onto your own wrist, push their wrist down and their elbow up. Notice that I am sitting straight with my legs wide, this gives me great stability and I can get extra leverage on Uke's wrist by lifting my hips up.

Outside of a friendly situation I do not need to worry so much about the other hand punching me, because we are aiming to break the arm as quickly as possible and move on to something else.

The easiest straight-arm lock has to be over the shoulder. Getting the Uke's palm facing upwards and their elbow just past your shoulder, pull their wrist down with one hand if you need to protect your head with the other (fig 1) or two hands for more power and an instant break (fig 2).

FIG 1

FIG 2

ARM & WRIST LOCKS

If Uke tries to lay flat still apply the lock but focus on pulling their wrist as though going under the your armpit.

47

The technique below is a lovely technique and can be used from a caught punch or from a grab, and standing up as well. The arm across the Uke's face keeps their head down and with a slight bend in the elbow you can put pressure on their throat, or just elbow them.

If you notice, my left arm across my body is bent and I am not holding on to the Uke's wrist to pull it down, as there isn't enough room to get enough power behind it. But with your arm bent you can use your elbow to apply pressure by pressing their arm towards the floor and sticking your chest up. Uke's arm is straight with the palm facing up. The other thing to point out is the bent leg next to Uke's body. This is bent to stop them gaining some control by pinning their leg across you.

This straight-arm lock below is very similar to the Waki Gatami (armpit lock on page 75) except your body is slightly further down the Uke's arm on to his elbow. Pull their wrist up with your hands. I like to wedge their arm up first by putting my elbow on the floor and trapping their wrist. This lock can be used when Uke is on all fours and you can pull the arm away and lock it, or it could start when stood up from a punch or a grab by bringing your arm over the top of the Uke's and sliding to the ground. It can be used as a pin or a break. For extra pain always grab hold of their fingers and pull towards their shoulder, thus applying a wrist locks as well.

ARM & WRIST LOCKS

The idea with the lock below is to break an attack by the Uke when trying to grab your lapel or punch you.

Take control of their wrist and turn on to your side simultaneously; then bring your leg over their arm and wedge your foot under the Uke's jaw or across their throat (perhaps kick them in the face as you do so). As you extend your leg and push the back of your knee through their elbow, the lock will be applied. If you keep your elbow on the mat and your forearm facing upwards this will give a nice bridge to your Uke's arm. Use your other foot to push the Uke's knee away to make them lay face down. Make sure they go down by kicking them in the groin.

You can aply the next lock very easily if you have the Uke trapped either with your legs hooked around their calfs, or around their waist.

Just take control and trap one of Uke's wrists and hold it with a monkey grip (thumb on the outside). As they pull away, bring your foot up and across their face and wedge it into their neck (top pic). To aply the lock simply straighten your leg.

If you're feeling confident and want to put them in even more pain try both legs, but this time push away with both legs and pull the wrists out to your shoulders.

ARM & WRIST LOCKS

This time I have got one leg on the outside and one leg on the inside (In the picture the left leg is on the outside and the right leg is on the inside). This is good for confusing the Uke. You can turn them over, prepare a kick to the throat or face, tie them up, or prepare the bottom leg (the right leg in the picture) to push and sweep the knee or to kick the groin or just to push and get some distance. Remember with the leg on the inside (the right one?) you will need to pull their arm towards your chest and NOT out to your shoulder.

With Uke's elbow over your thigh you can achieve a very basic straight-arm lock with possibilities to strangle/choke or to strike your opponent. I have got the forearm trapped under my armpit and am leaning on it slightly to apply pressure. In the pictures I am using the lock more as a pin so I can apply other techniques. My right leg is tucked in tight to the Uke's side to stop him moving away and my back is straight with my head out of the way of any strikes.

ARM & WRIST LOCKS

UDE GATAMI
ARM CRUSH

Moving on to Ude Gatame (arm crush), a lot of people get confused and think it's the same as the straight-arm lock but it isn't. The main difference is that you are stopping the wrist from moving and not moving it to break the arm. So keeping the wrist locked in and place pressure on the elbow, but pull it in with your hands or arms.

The picture below shows the two locks done at the same time – well done if you can get them on together (!) though this isn't expected, just for demonstration purposes.

As you can see, Uke's right arm is in Juji Gatame (straight-arm lock) where I am using the pivot of his elbow on my knee and pushing his wrist down. Uke's left arm is locked straight into the arm crush (Ude Garami) and I am using my hand to pull his elbow in. Normally from this position you would have Uke's other arm trapped and pull the elbow in with two hands. As shown opposite.

ARM & WRIST LOCKS

Another way of put the arm crush on is, with Uke on their front, trap their wrist into your shoulder and neck then pull their elbow into your body make sure you leave a gap between their arm and your body.

Ju ji Gatami (straight-arm lock) is often used in competitions as it is a safe arm lock and gives your opponent plenty of time to tap. However, if you leave a slight bend in the arm this will make the arm pop much quicker. The ideal angle is 135 degrees as that's where the arm is weakest, but depending on how much you are moving and the position you are in and the size of your opponent, anywhere around 135 will work, but be careful.

As you can see from the picture, Uke is in some pain :-)

I have got his hand close to my armpit pinning it in tight and I am lifting my right hip up and keeping the top half of my body flat. I am looking at Uke's elbow just to make sure it doesn't pop before he taps.

When Uke resists and tries to pull their arm back, pin the arm to your chest, try to keep your elbow in tight and touching the mat. To apply this lock very quickly kick your right leg over as if you are going to roll on your front, but keep the top half of your body flat on the mat.

ARM & WRIST LOCKS

This is the same principle but Uke has arm facing down. I'm holding on to his wrist and pulling it to the mat whilst pushing up with my hip. Uke will feel this on their elbow and also on their shoulder.

This time the lock is done from Kesa Gatami. By taking the arm from under Uke's head and controlling Uke's wrist you can get good leverage from this position and bring the elbow back for some elbow strikes to the head.

If you look at Uke's elbow you can see the Humorous bone popping out and the stress on the forearm and elbow.

The same lock with the same angle on the arm from Kesa Gatami (scarf hold): This time I am trapping Uke's wrist with my leg. I don't need to have my arm around his neck and I could trap his other arm instead. However, my left hand is free to strike or strangle. To apply the lock just push your foot down towards the mat and lift your thigh up.

This lock is similar to Ude Garami (figure four lock on page 57) but with the same angle as before. When applied properly you do not need to pull the arm down to Uke's waist as you would for the Ude Garami; just lift the arm under Uke's elbow slightly.

You could easily use this to take another position. Tate Shiho Gatame is one of the easiest as the lock would stay on through the transition.

UDE GARAMI
FIGURE FOUR, ENTANGLED LOCK

This lock is very common in competition because it's easy to set up, though it is a slow technique to apply. Key points to remember are to keep your weight on the Uke so that they don't lift their hip and counter the lock; keep the back of their wrist on the mat as you slide their arm down towards their hip and slightly lift up their elbow.

ARM & WRIST LOCKS

As with most locks there are many different ways to apply it. I personally prefer to keep my hand open and push down with the ridge hand on to the Uke's wrist/tendons. This seems to put the lock on a lot quicker. As you can see, the Uke's fingers have closed in, making the tendons in the arm tighter.

If Uke moves his arm out, this is to our favour because you can then apply the lock from page 56 much quicker.

If Uke straightens their arm then apply the straight-arm lock from page 42. This should all become instinct after practicing these locks for a while. You will obviously have your own favourite techniques but don't neglect the others or stop learning new ones.

If Uke pulls their arm in tight, then the lock will still work but you'll just need to lift their elbow up higher. Also you can put your elbow into the side of their neck for a strangle, or across their throat for a choke.

ARM & WRIST LOCKS

You can also change to just the one hand and strike or strangle with the other hand. By pulling their wrist down towards their shoulder (keeping it on the mat) and lifting their elbow up, this lock will go on extremely quickly with a lot of pain.

For a bit more pain, and also if Uke is lifting their hips to resist the lock, pull their wrist in so that Uke's knuckles are on the mat and their forearm is vertical. Then push their elbow towards their ear (it won't get that far, but if it does call an ambulance). You are focusing on putting your weight on to their knuckles and breaking their wrist.

If Uke is very flexible you can always release the hand holding your wrist and use it to push Uke's elbow forward. (This Uke isn't that flexible which is why his hips are so high, above).

If Uke manages to turn on to their side and bring their arm in, you can distract them for a second by placing your elbow on to their throat then apply the same wrist-breaking lock but this time you will need to concentrate more on pushing their wrist towards their knees to catch the knuckles on the floor and getting the forearm vertical. Like most locks this would need to be done quickly before Uke can roll you over.

ARM & WRIST LOCKS

Again, we are using the Ude Garami (figure four) hand positioning, but this time applying the wrist lock. Make sure that Uke's elbow is wedged against your body so it can't move, pull their hand back with the pressure placed mainly on their knuckles. Make sure you have a good strong base, one knee down and the other one up, this also gives you room to manipulate Uke's arm

If Uke is silly enough to try and sit up then you can just knock them back down with your elbow. To stop Uke punching you simply move your knee over and trap their free arm.

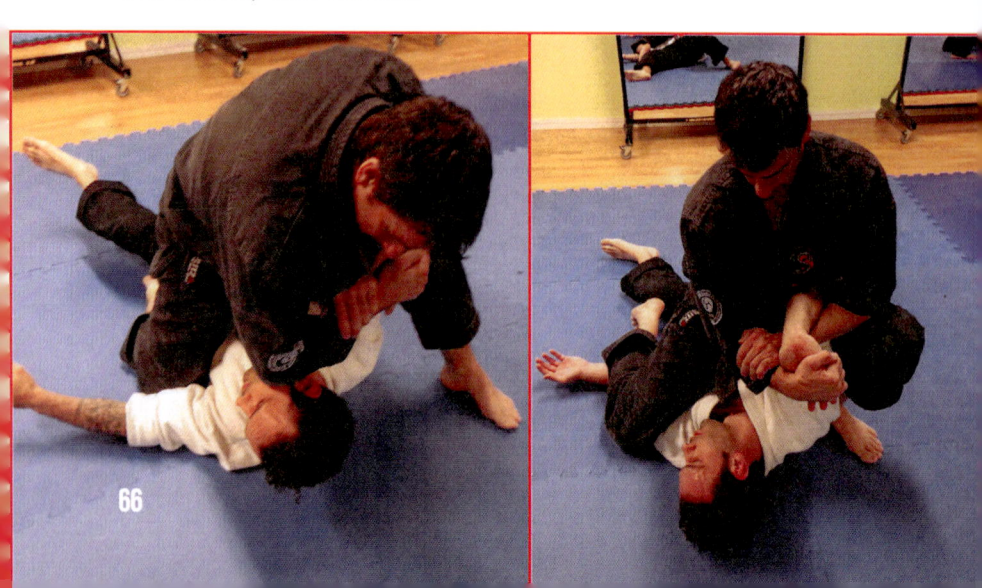

You might find that Uke tries to roll out, but don't panic as this will work in your favour. With Uke on their side they will not be able to strike you as long as their shoulder is on the mat and you keep weight on them. By stepping over their head and wedging your foot under their jaw you have a great pin for control and restraint.

ARM & WRIST LOCKS

We can quickly change this lock to the bent-arm lock and place the strangle on at the same time with the shin pushing into Uke's throat. Also from this position we could fall with our back on that mat for a straight-arm bar, but it's a bit pointless when we could finish the fight from our knees and still have the option to strike.

This is another version of the last lock but this time Uke's hand is the other way around, with the palm facing outwards. Focus on putting pressure on the knuckles and the fingers.

And again using your leg to stop any strikes.

If Uke tries to roll out, keep the lock on but force their hand behind them and keep their elbow where it is. Done quickly this will break the arm before they can roll back.

GYAKU UDE-GARAMI
REVERSE FIGURE FOUR, REVERSE ENTANGLED LOCK OR KIMURA

In cage/ring sports this lock is commonly called the Kimura due to the famous Judoka Masahiko Kimura defeating Helio Gracie, one of the founders of Brazilian Ju-Jitsu (BJJ), in 1951.

This lock is similar to Ude Garami but reversed. Uke's hand is now facing down towards their hips. So remembering the figure four technique, grab Uke's wrist and then bring your other hand underneath to grab your own wrist.

ARM & WRIST LOCKS

Then lift Uke up using the leverage from their arm and then slide your leg through and under them. You can then roll on your back, trap their legs with your own legs, and push their arm from one shoulder to the other. Keep it high and straight across their back – if their arm is too low or too high, it makes escaping much easier.

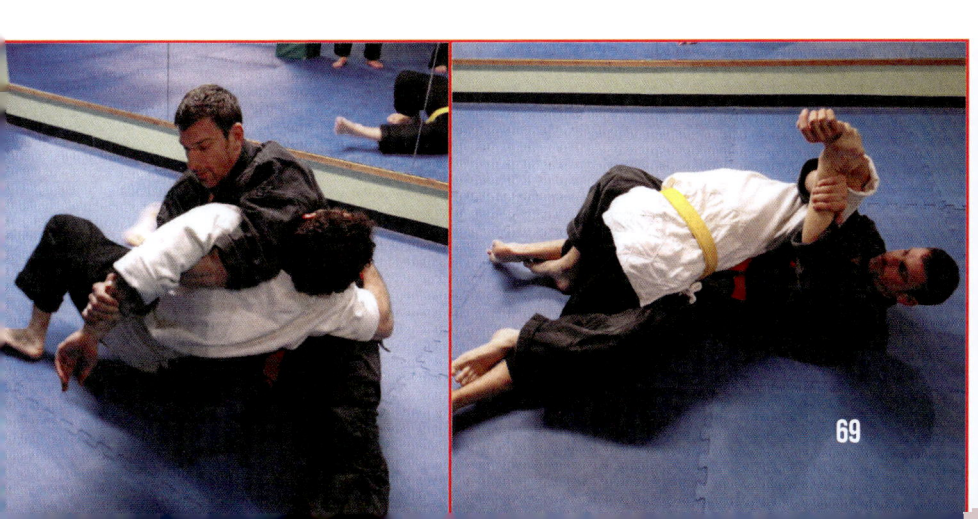

It can also be executed from the kneeling position by taking Uke's side and placing the lock on their arm. Once you have pulled them forward there is no way of Uke striking you or kicking you, but you must keep their body facing down so that they cannot roll out.

Ukes hand is on the floor, stopping his face from hitting the mat. This means that you know where both of his feet are (because you can see them) and their other hand. So once you are in this position there is no need to panic; just resume control and finish the technique. It doesn't matter if Uke's arm is out or they are trying to pull it in. If it's out, just carry on as before. If it's in then focus more on pushing their wrist along their back up towards their head.

So we have done Gyaku Ude-Garami from when Tori (the attacker) is on the top, and from the kneeling position, so now we'll look at it when Tori is on the bottom and Uke is on top. The first thing to do is to grab Uke's wrist; depending on what they are doing there are many ways of doing this. If they are striking you, have your guard up to your face and grab their wrist and force it straight to the floor (below left). This will pull their bodyweight forward. If they have both hands on your chest, grab hold of both of their wrists and pull off on to the floor (below, middle). You can wrap your legs around Uke to control them and push them back or to pull them forward with your legs. Now you'll need to get your other hand past the Uke's face, over the top of their arm, back under their arm and grab your own wrist. All without them moving or reacting (easy ;-)). Or we could take their mind off the fact that we are grabbing their wrist by striking their jaw on the way through or palm heeling their ear or holding their chin and applying a neck lock.

ARM & WRIST LOCKS

If they resist too much you can always let go of the wrist and hold their head and strike it.

Once you have finished playing and got the lock on you'll need to bring their head down to the floor, uncross your legs and roll your body into them, keeping their arm up and push it across to their opposite shoulder as before.

If Uke is strong and they fold their arm in tight, then let go with the hand that is holding your own wrist and grab the top of Uke's hand, pushing the knuckles in towards the wrist and then letting go with your other hand. Keep pulling the arm up to Uke's ear, this will apply the wrist lock, arm lock, shoulder lock and give you an opportunity to attack Uke's ribs. Keep your legs over the top of Uke's to stop them rolling out and escaping.

ASHI-SANKAKU-GARAMI
TRIANGULAR ENTANGLEMENT

It's one of those locks that looks awkward but once you've drilled it ten times or more, it just flows. The first thing to do is grab Uke's wrist, either from them punching or grabbing you, and then in one fluid motion bring your leg up on to their arm (just above the elbow) and all the way over so that Uke's face is on the floor.

ARM & WRIST LOCKS

If Uke is strong and resisting at this point you can always go for Ju Ji Gatami (straight-arm lock)

So now that you have Uke face down bring your leading leg (the leg that is doing all of the work) under your other leg and bring it up behind your knee, then sit up.

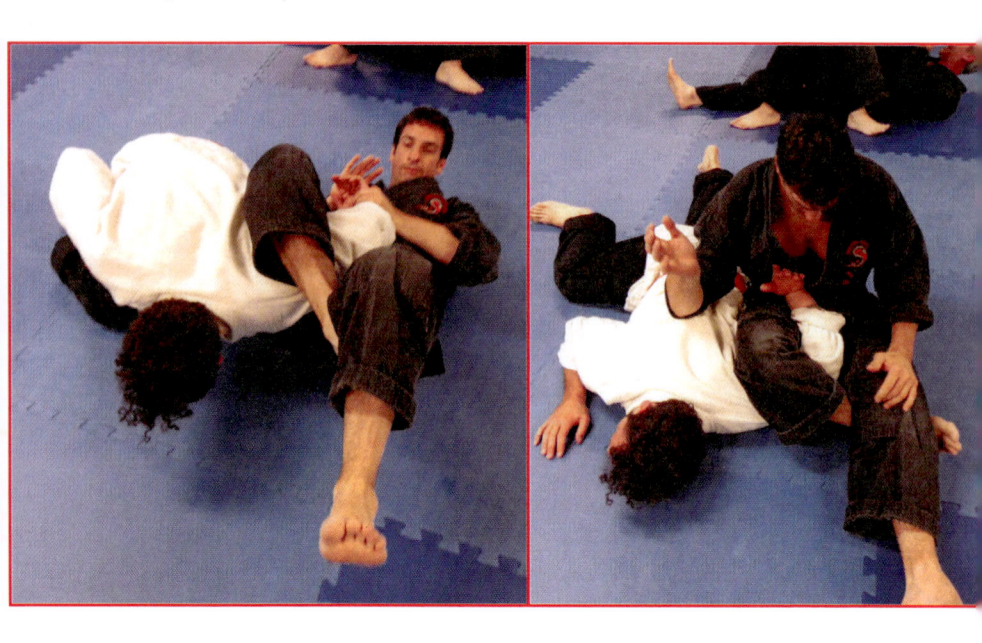

If Uke's arm is not bent yet then just pull the wrist round so that the back of their hand is against your body, then all you'll need to do is roll forward causing pain to the shoulder and the wrist. If you find it hard to go forward then push yourself up by placing your hand on Uke's back. If Uke tries to get up, force them back down with your elbow in their spine.

WAKI GATAMI
ARMPIT LOCK

This can be done from a punch or if Uke is trying to grab you. From a punch take the wrist with both hands and carry the punch through. Bring your outside elbow over the arm and pin it to the floor.

ARM & WRIST LOCKS

Once Uke is on the floor plant your elbow on to the mat, keep Uke's arm straight and keep your legs wide. With your arm locked in all you need to do is sink your armpit down and slightly lift your wrist up. To add a bit more pain pull the wrist back and push their knuckles into their forearm or grab their fingers and push their wrist forward and again into the forearm.

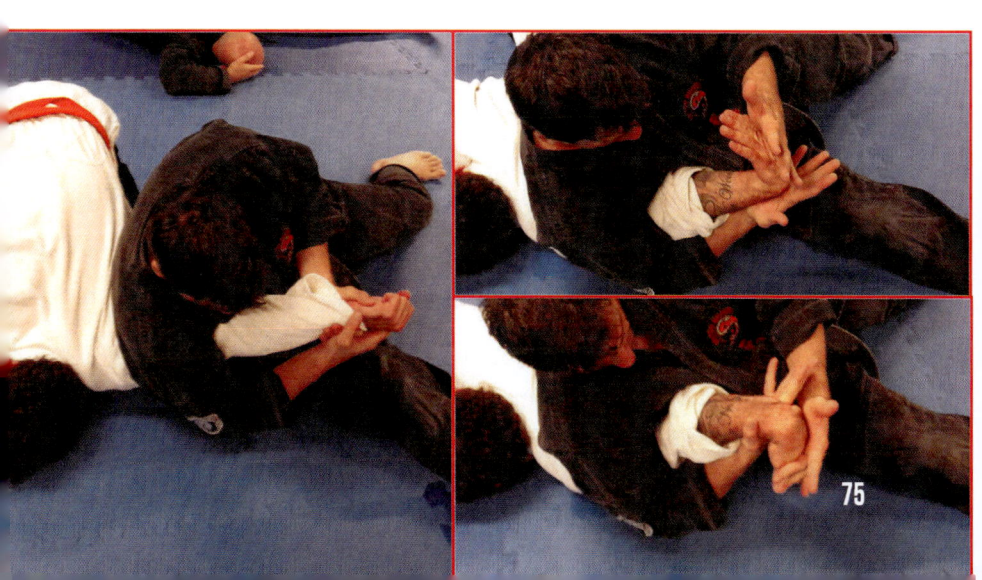

From this initial punch or grab you could also go straight into a straight-arm lock simply by moving your elbow on to the back of Uke's elbow. Keep hold of Uke's wrist with both hands and keep their arm straight, then force them down with your elbow.

HIZA UDE GATAMI
KNEE ARM LOCK

From Uke grabbing your lapel, take hold of their wrist and fall backwards on to your side, pulling them forward. As you're doing this, place one knee under their shoulder and the other on top of their shoulder.

ARM & WRIST LOCKS

Make sure that your bottom foot is tucked around Uke's side and that your top leg is across their back, knee on their shoulder, and your foot on the opposite hip. To apply the lock, lift the arm up and push your knee down. The wrist lock can be simply added, too.

UDE-HISHIGI-WAKI-GATAME
LYING BACK ARMPIT LOCK

From Uke grabbing your lapel, take hold of their wrist and fall backwards on to your side, pulling them forward. As you're doing this, place one knee under their shoulder and the other on top of their shoulder.

Make sure that your bottom foot is tucked around Uke's side and that your top leg is across their back, knee on their shoulder, and your foot on the opposite hip. To apply the lock, lift the arm up and push your knee down. The wrist lock can be simply added, too.

USHIRO UDE GARAMI
HAMMER LOCK

From Uke grabbing your lapel, take hold of their wrist and fall backwards on to your side, pulling them forward. As you're doing this, place one knee under their shoulder and the other on top of their shoulder.

ARM & WRIST LOCKS

Make sure that your bottom foot is tucked around Uke's side and that your top leg is across their back, knee on their shoulder, and your foot on the opposite hip. To apply the lock, lift the arm up and push your knee down. The wrist lock can be simply added, too.

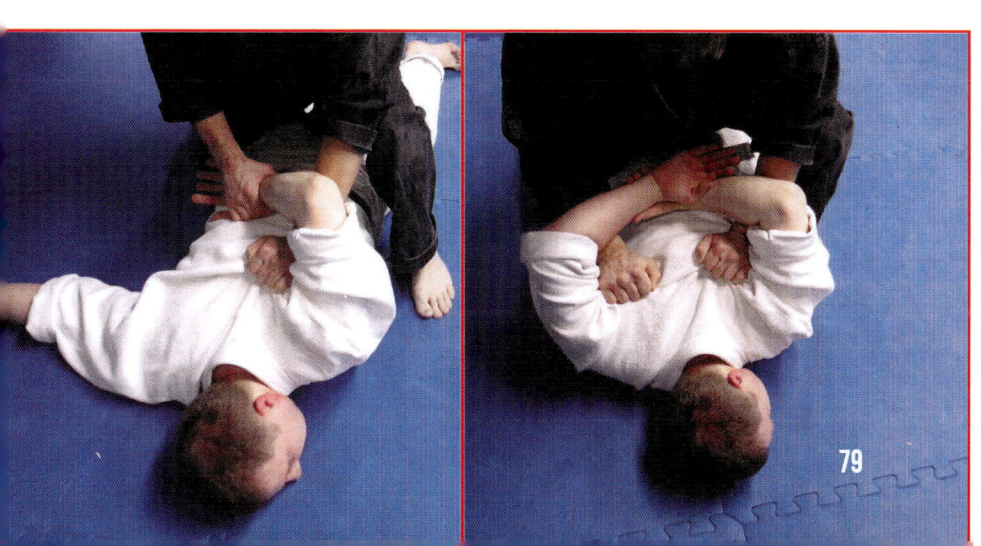

KATA WAZA
SHOULDER LOCK

You'll need to get Uke on their side (you are kneeling) for this technique, from either a throw or by manipulating them on the ground. Once you have Uke on their side you'll need to place one leg over their waist and pull your heel into their body as tight as you can. Trap Uke's hand between your bicep and ribs and bring your hands together on to their elbow. All you need to do now is turn your body and Uke's elbow towards their head, let your arm and body move as one.

Obviously if Uke is fighting back a lot or can resist this lock, you can always strike them and full back into Ju Ji Gatami, or you can work a strangle in by using their lapels, which are in easy reach, and their neck is open.

TEKUBI GATAMI
WRIST LOCKS

Most wrist locks can be applied very easily and some are a little more complicated, but the quickness to apply them and the fact you don't need a lot of room means they are a must-have in your arsenal.

The wrist has six main movements, which I'll explain. Put your hand straight in front of you, palm facing down. The first movement is Extension, moving the wrist so that your fingers are pointing up; the second is Flexion – fingers are down; third is Ulnar Deviation, where the wrist moves to the outside of the body; fourth is Radial Deviation – wrist moves to the inside of the body; firth is Pronation, the wrist moves thumb down; and the 6th, or Supination, sees the little finger move down. The last two really work the two bones in the forearm (Ulna and Radius). With none of these movements (unless you are extremely flexible or double jointed) does the hand touch the forearm, which means the wrist can be broken at all of these angles.

There are ten small bones in the wrist and numerous tendons, ligaments and fasciae, which is why wrist locks are so much more painful then arm or leg locks.

ARM & WRIST LOCKS

The easiest wrist lock is done from the Uke grabbing your lapel. Now secure their hand with your (diagonally opposite hand) and press it at the wrist so their palm is on your chest. You can use two hands if you wish. Now turn your shoulders 90 degrees from the Uke and the lock will be applied.

Keep their hand tight and close to your chest.

WRIST LOCKS CONTINUED

These next few locks are commonly used in Ju Jitsu but very rarely used in groundwork, which is a shame because they work really well when the Uke is close to you. You can practice these techniques standing up or on the ground. You obviously have limited room to move about on the floor but you can control your opponent more with your legs and gravity plays a big part, too. As these locks go on, Uke will naturally want to fall on to you, causing them more pain.

The first one is **Kotegaeshi** (turning wrist lock). When applied standing up the lock can turn into a very effective throw. So, keeping that in mind, when we apply it in groundwork we can simply break the wrist or use it as a means to turn Uke over onto their back.

KOTEGAESHI
TURNING WRIST LOCK

As Uke comes in to punch, strangle or grab you, cover up to protect yourself and to disguise what you are about to do. Grab their hand and twist it so their palm faces towards them; with your other hand place it along their little finger and push/twist their hand round further. Put your leg on the same side they turn to, in order to stop them rolling away.

If you want to roll them on to their back, bring that leg down but bring the other leg up and kick them over at the same time as putting the lock on.

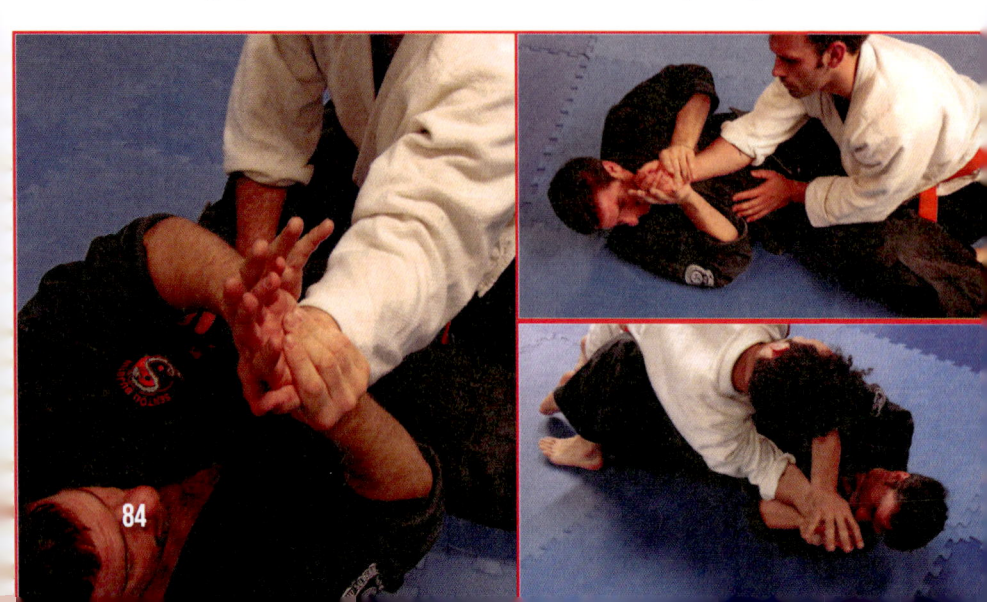

IKKYO

For many styles of Ju Jitsu this is the first to learn, hence the name. With Uke grabbing your lapel or going for a one-handed strangle, bring your hand across Uke's face (you can strike on the way through if you wish) and grab their wrist as far around it as you can, putting your middle finger in the crease of their wrist. Your elbow should be pointing up. Now twist their wrist back towards the direction your hand came from and bring your elbow back down. You can now use your other hand for more strength

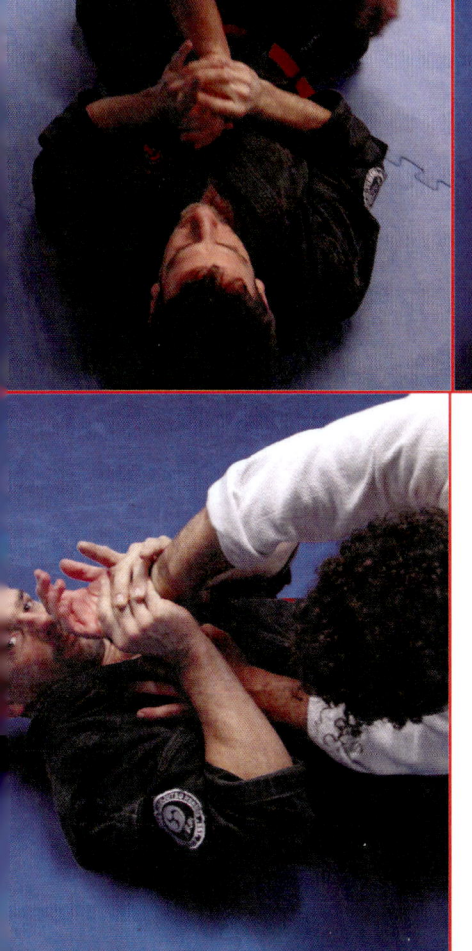

ARM & WRIST LOCKS

When using this lock standing up, keep the back of their hand on your chest; but when on the ground, you will run out of room so you can lift up (push the hand away) and twist, keeping your leg around Uke to stop them moving too far.

NIKKYO

Start off the same way as Ikkyo but don't bring Uke's wrist around as far, preferably with their knuckles on your chest, and have a slight bend in their arm but keep the tension on. Now with your other hand place your middle finger in the crease of their elbow and bring both of your elbows slowly down to the floor, keep the grip tight.

SANKYO

With Sankyo you'll need to have Uke's thumb pointing towards your face. You can do this from the start of Ikkio or Nikkio after twisting it around. Interlock your thumb web (or 'Purlicue') with Uke's. Then twist their hand inwards towards their face, place your other hand on their elbow with your thumb in the crease of the elbow to stop the hand sliding off and try to keep their arm at 90 degrees.

ARM & WRIST LOCKS

YONKIO

Yonkio is another simple wrist lock working on where the wrist has limited movement (side to side). When holding Uke's hand with their little finger pointing upwards, hold one hand close to their wrist, putting the whole hand under control. Now force their hand up pushing their fingers towards their face.

ULNAR DEVIATION OUTSIDE

The second way is to lift the wrist up and guide Uke's finger towards their armpit. On both of these locks keep the wrist straight and don't let it fold in.

Holding Uke's hand in this position will work the lock in the up and down position if you are standing up.

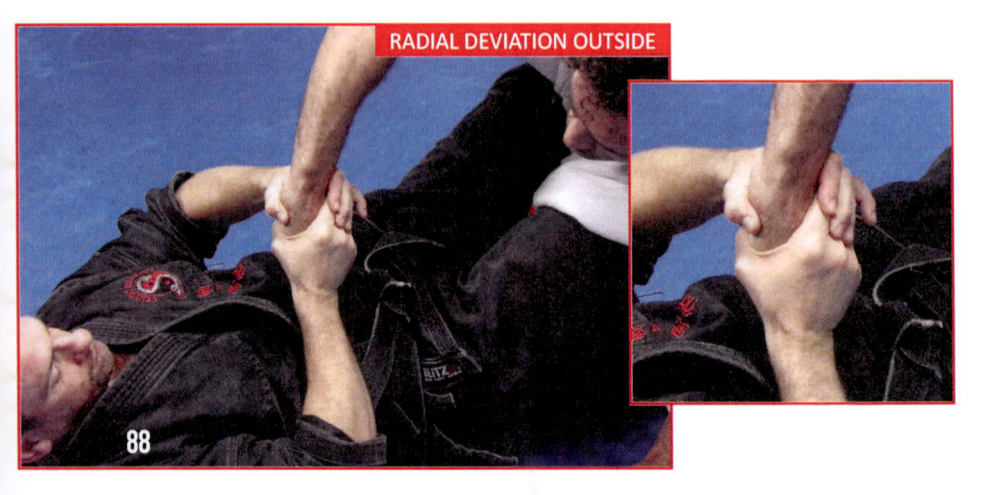

RADIAL DEVIATION OUTSIDE

SHEIO-NAGE

As the name suggests when standing up this lock is normally finished with a throw by twisting the arm up high and turning Uke so that you are back to back, then pulling the arm back down to leaver Uke on to their back.

The trick to doing this on the ground is to grab Uke's arm as far around from underneath as possible, then twist it until your palm is facing down. You will feel the tension on their arm and see their body start to turn. To keep the tension/pain on, place your hand just above their elbow to keep the right angle on.

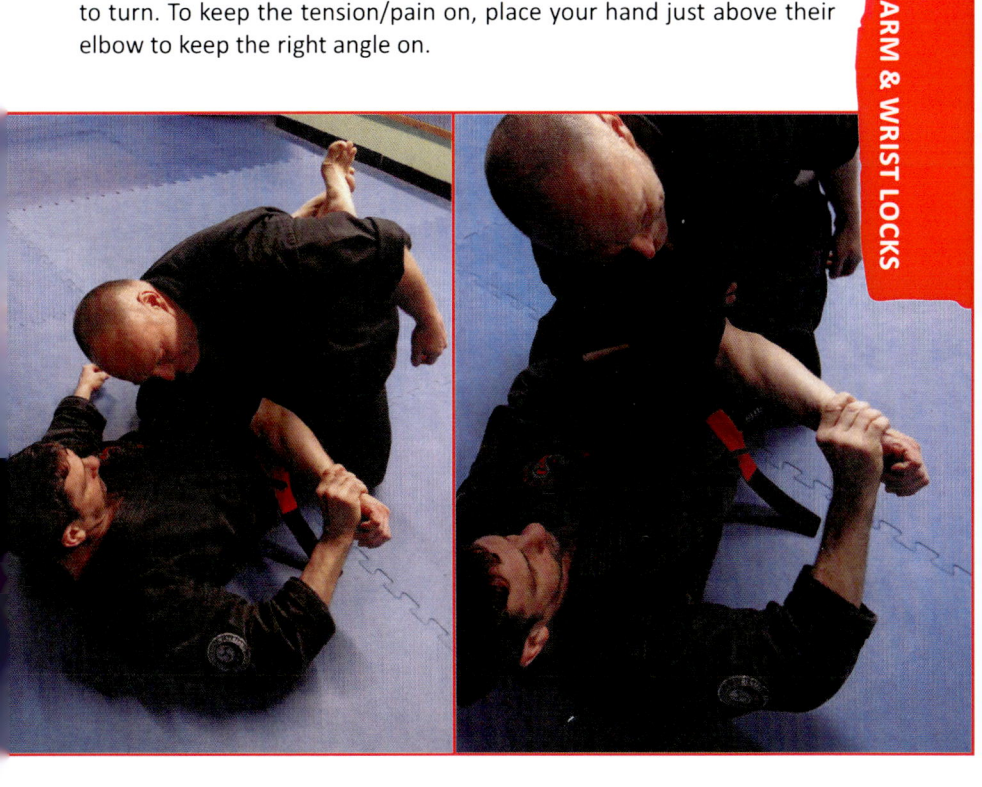

ARM & WRIST LOCKS

You can see the twist and tension on Uke's arm. It puts pressure on the wrist, forearm, elbow and shoulder.

89

TEKUBI GATAMI
MASTER LOCK, HYPER FLEXING WRIST LOCK

The easiest way to practice this lock is to start from Ikkio. As you turn Uke's wrist and their thumb pops up, grab it seeing that your thumb is essentially uppermost, between their thumb and fingers.

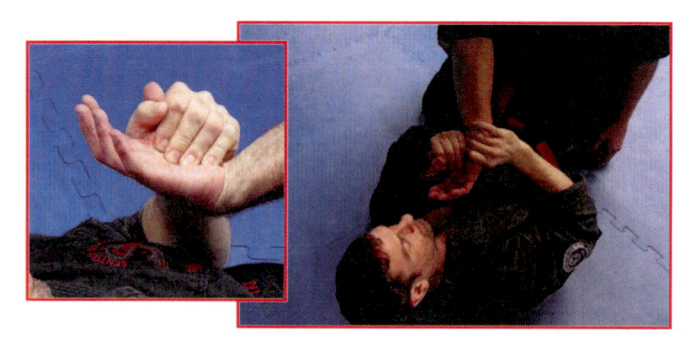

Then circle their wrist around so their fingers are pointing outside of their body, but you MUST make sure that Uke's knuckles are trapped by being curled into your wrist.

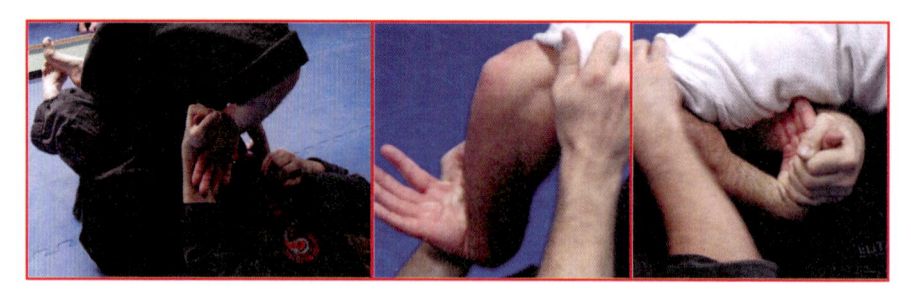

Carry that motion on until the lock is on and Uke is screaming and tapping like a fish on a boat. (see below)

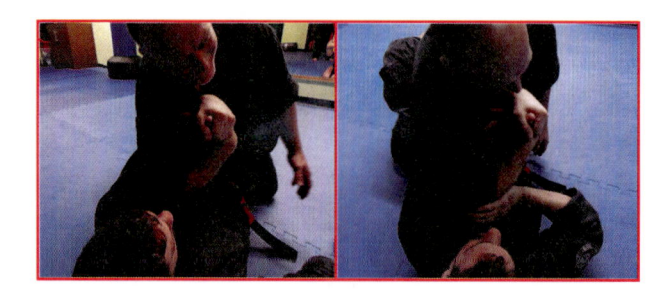

BENT WRIST LOCK

You can apply this lock in a friendly or non-friendly way. It's basically a the figure four hand position again to lift Uke up, or you can fall back into the Ju ji Gatami position with this wrist lock on. The not-so-nice way is to keep Uke's wrist in the same position, but take the hand out that is holding your own arm and place it on your other hand and pulling Uke's knuckles back to their forearm.

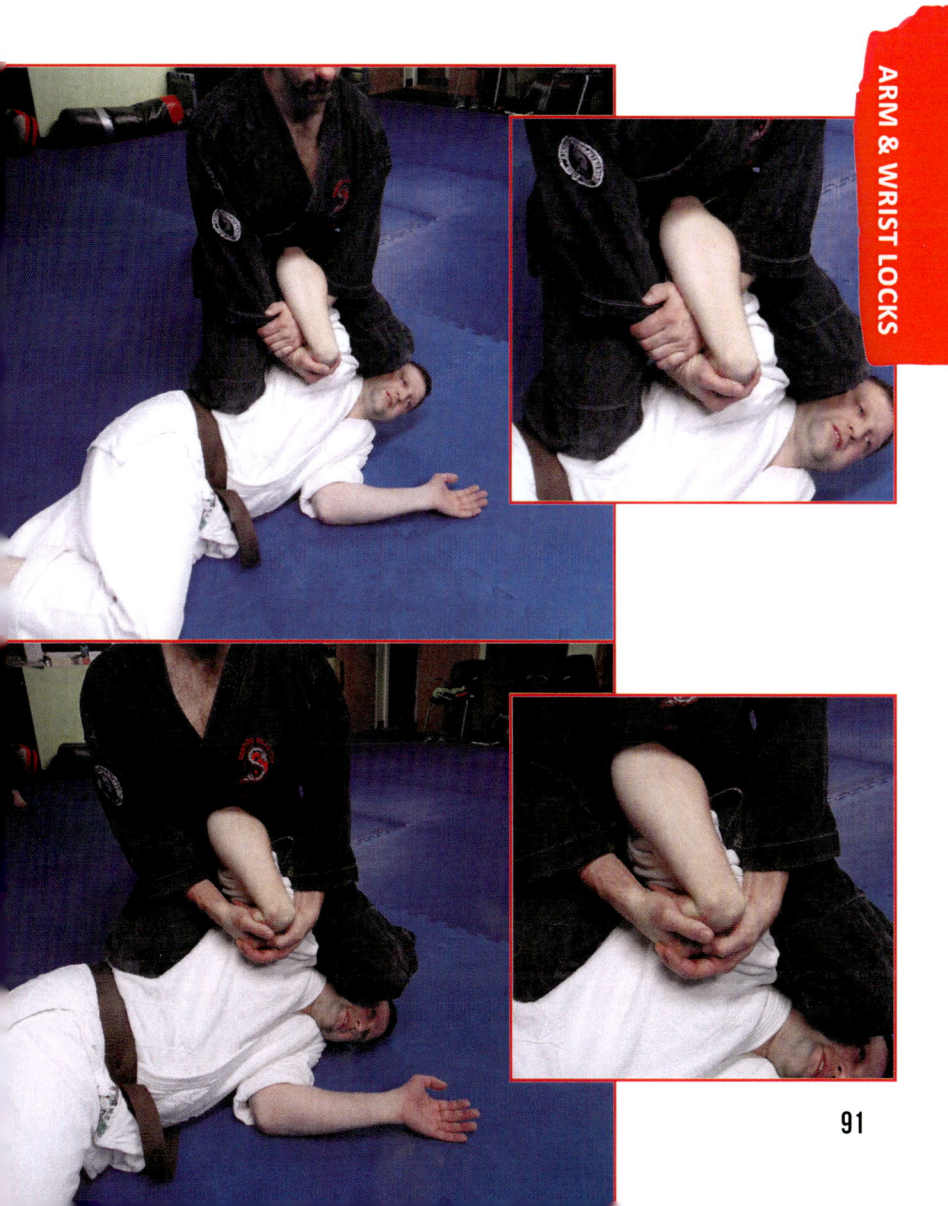

ARM & WRIST LOCKS

Another variation of the bent wrist lock (or 'goose neck') shown here is with Uke and Tori in the kneeling position. First of all curl your arm over Uke's arm, their Tricep in your armpit, and clasp your forearm, putting your other hand on top of theirs to adopt the figure four hand position.

Then lift Uke's arm up but keep your weight on their Tricep (this will keep the weight on Uke so that they can't lift their other hand to strike with, without falling down). Bring it up against your chest and pull their knuckles towards you to apply the lock.

SHOTIE GATAMI
PALM WRIST LOCK

A very simple lock in which the palm of Uke is flat on your chest as if they are trying to push themselves off of you. Placing one or two hands on Uke's elbow, push their arm into your chest. You don't want to come too far up on to the elbow otherwise you will end up pushing Uke's hand down and freeing it. Trap Uke's legs so that they can't roll forward and roll out.

ARM & WRIST LOCKS

There is another wrist lock that would work well on a stubborn Uke who is resisting Ju Ji Gatami (some people are just like that!). Bring your leg up and trap Uke's wrist with your calf. Although you can put your foot across their throat or heal in their wind pipe, the finishing technique is to put your foot under Uke's neck, and as you straighten your leg, the lock will go on. You can use your hand to help pull your leg up, to strike or to keep your balance.

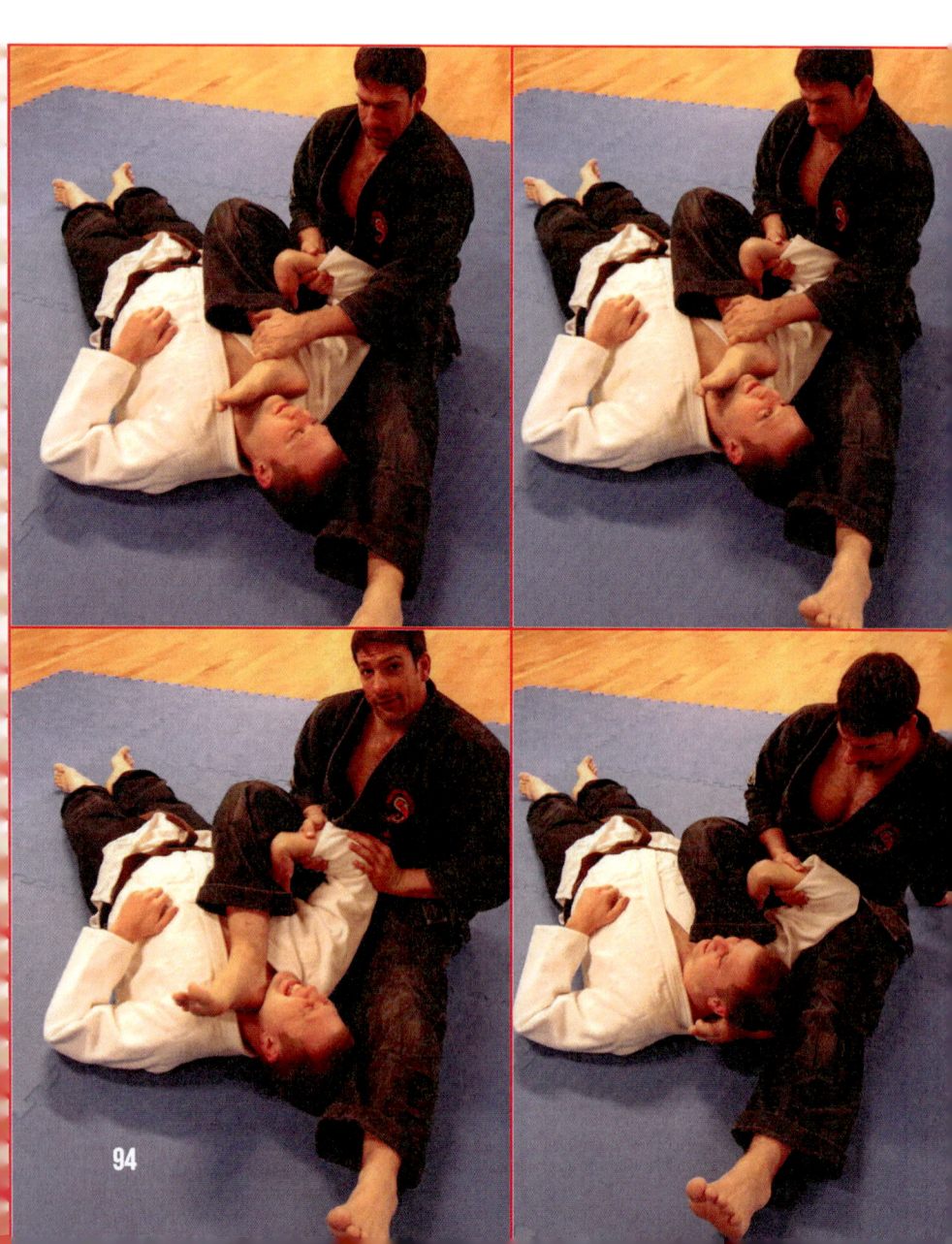

Also from this position you can put on another variation of Kata Waza (shoulder lock) by releasing Uke's arm and bringing your hand underneath the arm to grab their wrist. Keep Uke's arm out (but not straight) so that they can't bring it in towards their head.

As you can see it's extremely hard to get out of. Even if you feel a sneeze coming, Uke still can't escape!

ARM & WRIST LOCKS

If you look at Uke's elbow in the last picture it's right next to my knee, so a quick change of hand position and you can put on Ju Ji Gatami. Push Uke's hand towards their body and bring your knee towards the ground to apply the lock.

BICEP LOCK

This lock works on the same principle as the knee dislocation (see page 98). Bring your calf over the Uke's bicep and wedge it into the crease of their elbow; then push their forearm forward to trap your leg tight in their arm.

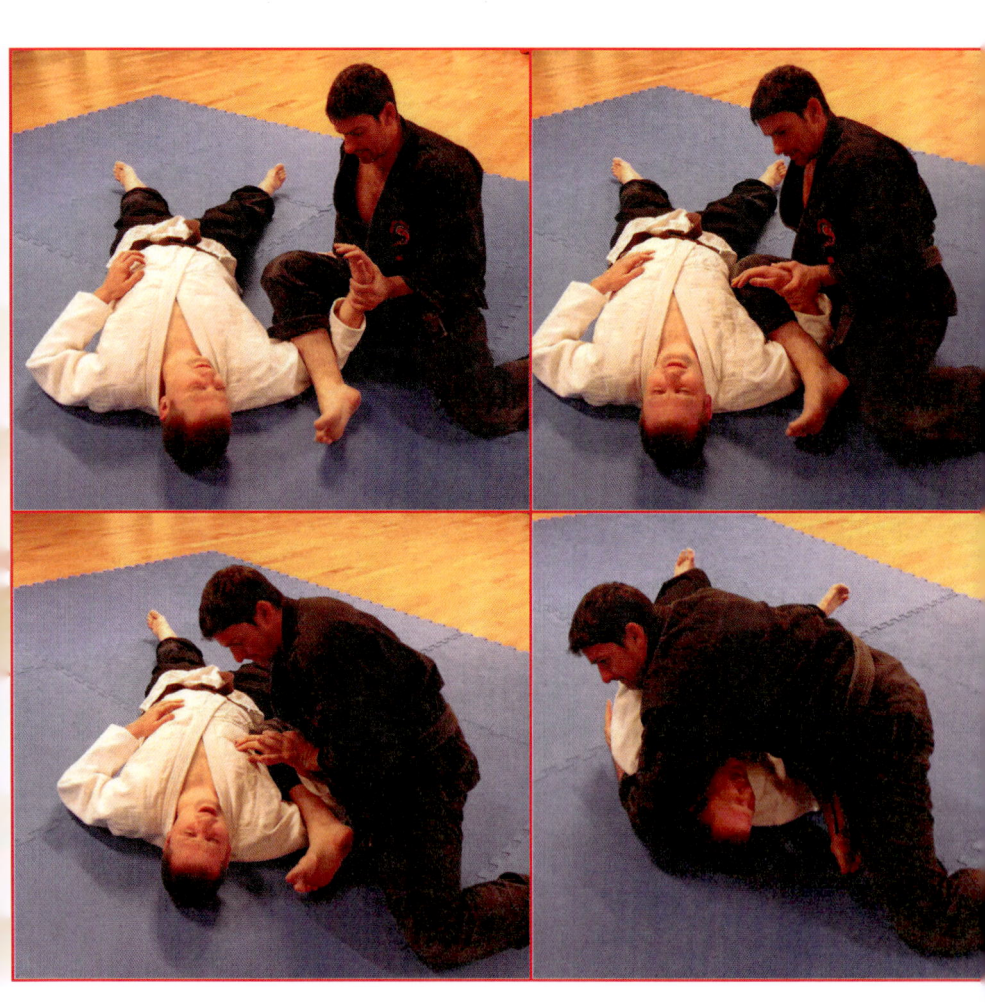

As you lean forward you can grab hold of the Uke and pull yourself in really tight. As your shin cuts into the Uke's bicep it will cause them lots of pain. But b aware of their free hand and take control of it as soon as possible.

ASHI GATAMI
LEG/FOOT LOCKS

Leg /foot locks are imperative to groundwork: It doesn't matter what position you are in, you can attack someone literally from head to toe. Some leg locks require a bit more strength than others because legs are obviously stronger than arm; but remember technique is always the key to getting the Uke to tap out. In Japan the word for leg and foot are the same ('Ash') so the names could be a bit confusing to start with but you will remember them eventually.

When applying leg locks always keep your eye on Uke's other leg, which could kick or heal you, and on their hands for strikes.

NIPPON-ASHI-HISHIGI
SINGLE LEG CRUSH/DISLOCATION / CALF LOCK

This is a very common lock focusing on using the blade of your arm to cut into Uke's calf. It's the figure-four hand position again. With this lock try and focus on lifting up the Uke's knee and keeping their shin horizontal; when their hip leaves the floor, the pain should go on and there is no way for them to hit or kick you. If they try to kick you, twist the leg you are holding into the kicking leg.

If Uke tries to pull their leg out, don't panic – just let the leg slide out as far as their heel, and when their heel touches your forearm, lock it back on. Concentrate on the blade of your forearm cutting into Uke's Achilles heel, and if that doesn't work, just lean backwards, bending the Uke's toes.

From the calf lock (see page 98), if Uke tries to roll out let them roll on to their side and then apply the knee lock with the same figure-four hand position. Let Uke's leg roll through your arms until you can place your hand on the side of their knee. Now you need to lock Uke's foot in tight and push down on their knee. For more strength lean your body forward slightly – not too much in case Uke pulls you forward, off balance.

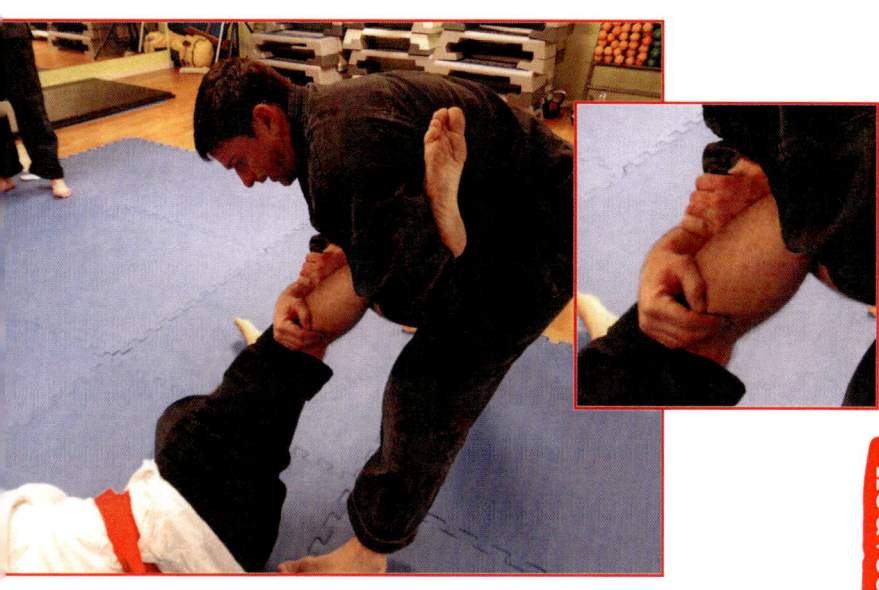

Or you could follow Uke all the way around until they are on their front, again by just letting their leg slide through your hands. Once they are on their front, keep your back straight, bring one leg up so that your foot stabilizes you, giving you the height to lift Uke's leg up; then focus on making their knee leaving the floor straight upwards, but don't lean back.

LEG & FOOT LOCKS

For an extra bit of pain trap Uke's other leg with your leg and pull it across and under the leg you are holding.

Or you can apply **Ryo-Ashi-Hishi (double-leg dislocation)** by grabbing both legs at the same time. Remember to have one of your legs up, both for stability and to gain height to apply the technique. Start the technique by leaning forward and holding the legs then sit up and straighten your back.

ASHI-DORI-GARAMI
ENTANGLED LEG DISLOCATION

This technique can be used as a pin, or to pop the knee out. With the Uke on their front, fold one of their legs into the crease of their other leg, then push the other leg up to trap the first leg. For more pressure, use your chest to lean on the upwards-pointing leg and you can even grab Uke's collar to pull you downwards even closer.

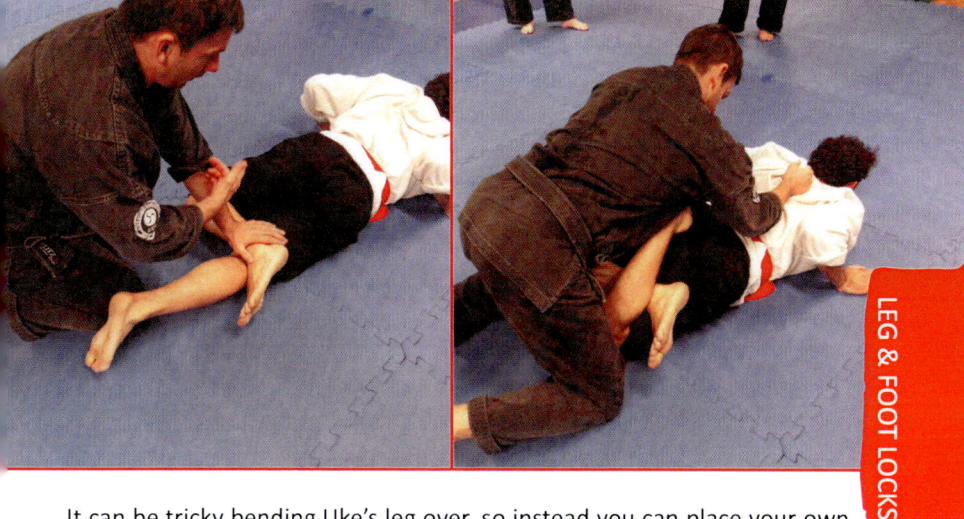

It can be tricky bending Uke's leg over, so instead you can place your own arm into the crease of Uke's leg. The only disadvantage is that your arm is trapped, but the Uke is pinned on their front and won't be able to attack.

LEG & FOOT LOCKS

HIZA GATAMI
STRAIGHT-KNEE LOCK

There are a few basic ways to apply this lock. The first is like Ju Ji Gatami (straight-arm lock), where – after throwing the Uke – you take hold of a leg and spin around.

Once you are at 90 degrees to Uke, place one foot on Uke's other leg to control and stretch it, and bring your knees in closer. The trick is to twist your hips towards Uke's feet and twist the top half of your body in the other direction. Make sure that your knee is tight to Uke's and that their foot is pointing towards their head.

Another way is to hug Uke's leg as if in the fetal position and lying on your side, and then straighten your body to apply the lock.

Another variation is to turn the other way once you have hold of Uke's leg and sit as close to Uke's head as possible whilst keeping hold of their leg. Use your left leg to take control of Uke's left leg and hold on to their heel.

LEG & FOOT LOCKS

Like all locks they are supposed be applied quickly. This one is no exception and most Ukes tap out before the technique is properly finished. With my right knee up I want to bring Uke's knee across my thigh and pull the heel down to break the leg, but most of the time the Uke taps before this happens because of the pulling and tearing of the groin muscles and tendons.

HIZA-HISHIGI
KNEE CRUSH/DISLOCATION

This lock is a simple matter of leverage. Again, once you have thrown Uke hold on to the heel of their foot, turn so that you are facing the same way as them, then drop to one knee (making sure that Uke's knee is touching your thigh). As you drop pull the heel up.

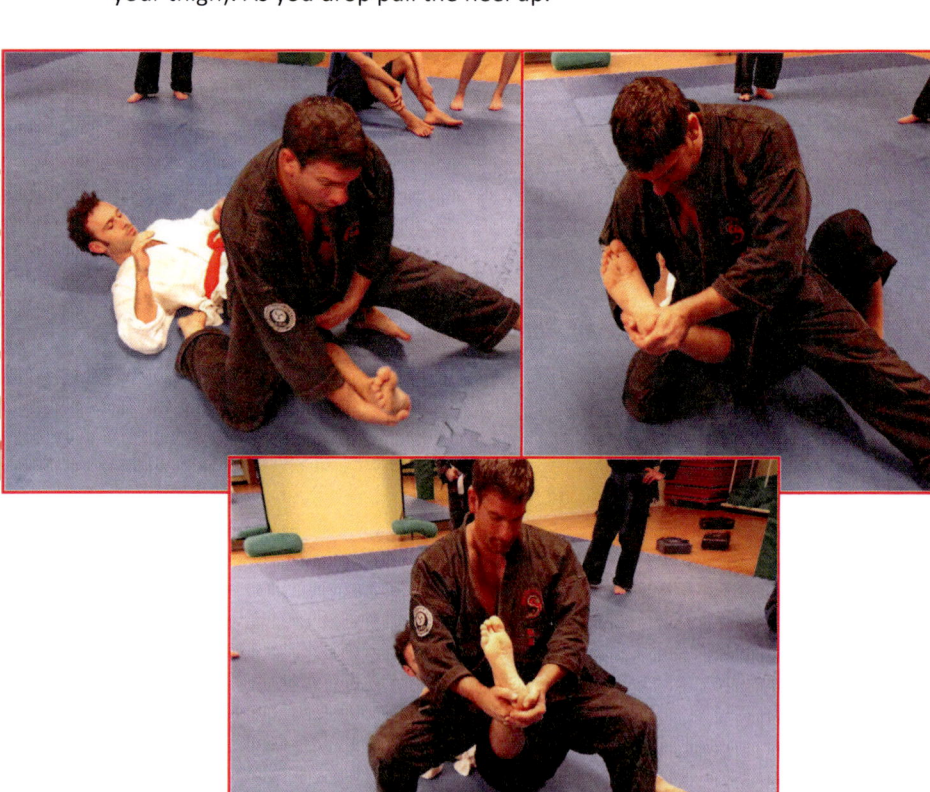

Keep one leg out for stability. Or you could stay up and squat down in a Kiba Dachi – the 'Sumo stance' – whilst pulling the heel up. Make sure that Uke's knee is on your inner thigh because if you lift the leg straight up, there will be pain but it won't be the Uke feeling it…!

ASHI GATAMI
FOOT LOCK/CRANK

Once again the figure-four hand position is used, with one arm under Uke's calf and the other hand pushing their toes and foot straight back.

Lifting Uke's leg up to keep their hip off of the floor prevents them from punching you or kicking hard. You can apply the lock so that it works on either side of the foot. If Uke's shin is touching your ribs and their foot is horizontal in front of you, you can still apply it by pushing their toes downwards.

LEG & FOOT LOCKS

ASHI GAKE
FOOT/HEEL HOOK

The trick with this lock is to make sure that Uke's leg is properly trapped. There are a few different ways to apply this. You can use your wrist or forearm under the heel or even grab the heel with one hand and the toes with the other hand and twist the same way. In the first picture I have a loose leg grip for a couple of reasons; one because I want to break something quick and don't want to faff about worrying about my legs; another is so that I can kick Uke easily to the groin or stomach. Some competition guys like to cross their own legs to stop Uke leg from sliding out, especially if Uke is sweaty. To apply the lock you can pull Uke's heel towards your face or twist your hips and legs towards the floor and twist your body the opposite way.

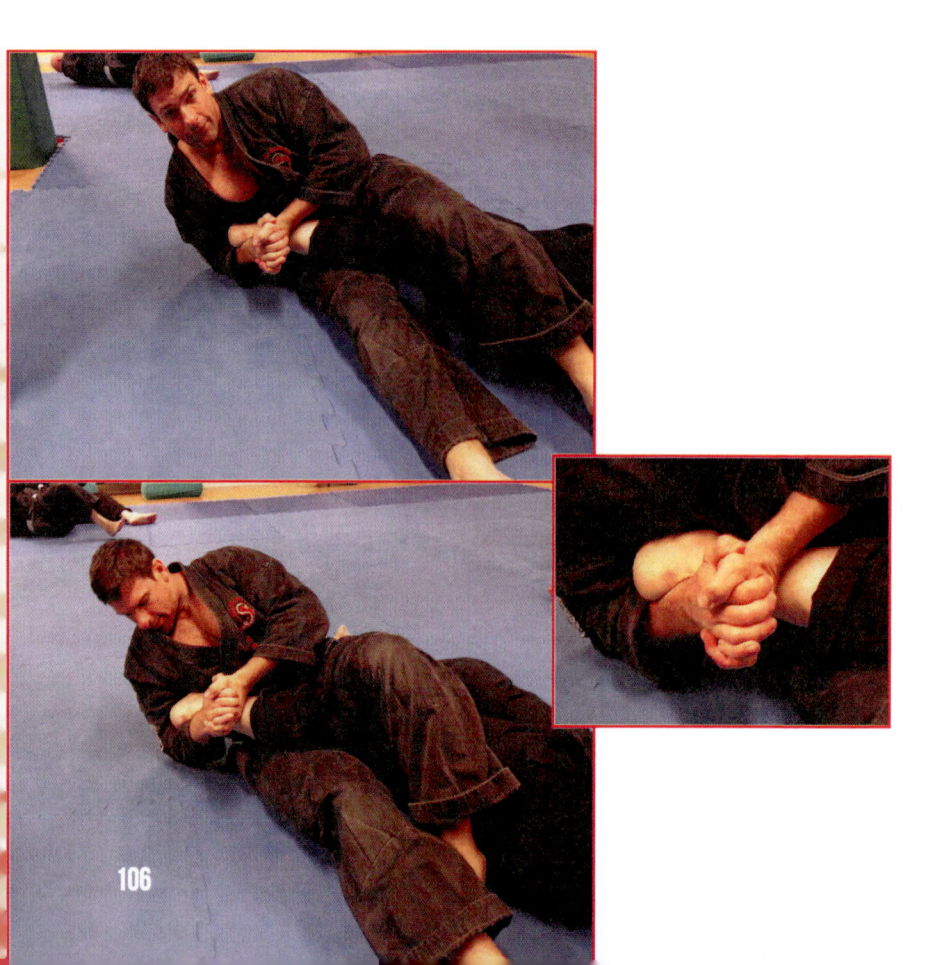

HIZA GATAMI
KNEE LOCK

This lock is quick and simple. Lift Uke's leg up or – if you have just thrown them – keep hold of it and place your foot next to Uke's hip and place your shin across their knee. Obviously this is meant to be very quickly applied, but done slowly when practising. Done slowly, it can be a little tricky, but works a treat when needed.

LEG & FOOT LOCKS

TATE-SHIHO-HIZA-HISHIGI
DISLOCATION OF THE KNEE IN 8TH IMMOBILIZATION

This technique is done when Uke is on top of you and trapped between your legs, trying to get in to Tate Shiho Gatami. Bring your legs over the top of Uke's and hook your feet under their shins. Take control of the top half of their body and then stretch out as far as you can to apply the lock.

ASHI TORI GARAMI
FOOT ENTANGLEMENT

The last leg/foot lock is applied when Uke is behind you and attempting to apply a single wing or rear strangle. If Uke doesn't have a lot of experience they may well cross their legs to take more control of you, but what they should do is place their legs inside yours and force them apart. This will give them more stability and stop the lock from going on. To apply the lock, when Uke's legs are crossed, simply bring one leg over the top of Uke's feet; then your other leg across your foot, and then push out. As you can see by the Uke's face (face pulling is optional but Nick is keen to participate) , this is a very painful lock, so be careful and enjoy it! If you are not very flexible you can always hold your leg to pull it up. Also if you feel threatened by Uke's choke, hold on to their forearm with the monkey grip (thumb and fingers together) keep your elbow in tight and pull down.

SHIME WAZA
CHOKES AND STRANGLES

This chapter is on strangles, chokes and neck cranks. They are all extremely dangerous so extreme caution must be taken.

The deference between a strangle and a choke is simple but many people confuse them.

Think 'Blood' and 'Air'. A strangle cuts off the blood supply to the brain by pushing on the archeries either side of the neck; a choke puts pressure on the wind pipe/throat. A strangle can put somebody unconscious and a choke can kill them by causing the throat to swell up and stopping the person from breathing. This could be instant or take some time – so be aware. If someone has been choked badly make sure they are not home alone after training and that they can swallow fine; any doubts whatsoever, take them to the hospital. I'm talking from experience here. A choke can also damage the voice box, so any changes in a person's voice, go to the hospital.

A neck crank is basically bending the neck into a place is doesn't want to go or can't go, so it could cause a broken neck which could paralyse Uke or kill them.

Take all of the following techniques very slow and make sure Uke knows to tap when they feel any discomfort.

THE NECK

1) The Sternocleidomastoid muscle turns the head. If damaged it can cause stiff/sore neck, blurred vision, headaches or dizziness.

2) Carotid artery; arteries are the circulatory system's blood vessels responsible for carrying newly oxygenated blood from the heart throughout the rest of the body.

3) The thyroid cartilage ('Adams Apple')

4) Jugular vein; veins are the circulatory system's blood vessels that return blood from the body to the heart.

5) The trachea ('windpipe')

CHOKES & STRANGLES

HADAKA JIME
REAR NAKED CHOKE

Hadaka Jime, or naked choke, is so called due to the fact it is applied without using the Gi and is one of the easiest chokes and probably one of the most dangerous due to the speed it can be applied and the fact that it attacks the trachea. If the technique is prepared a few inches away from your attacker's throat and pulled in quickly you are basically striking their throat with a lot of power. Because their back is against your chest they have nowhere to go. So with that in mind make sure the blade of your arm is on Uke's throat first, then very slowly pull in.

Bring your forearm across Uke's trachea/throat and join hands (palms together) keep your forearm straight pull into your chest very slowly.

You can keep Uke's head from moving by pushing your head onto theirs.

Another version is, instead of joining hands, you put your forearm across Uke's throat as before and hold your bicep, then bend that arm and place your hand behind Uke's head. Always make sure that Uke's back is against your chest. Take a breath in to inflate your chest then squeeze both arms in slowly.

CHOKES & STRANGLES

HADAKA JIME
NAKED STRANGLE

This is another version often seen in cage/ring sports as it is safer to apply and gives Uke time to tap. It uses the same principle as the last technique but the arm that comes round Uke's neck comes around a bit further so that your elbow is down Uke's centre line. This changes the technique from a choke to a strangle. Modern martial artists often gets this wrong.

As you can see from the first picture my body is turned off to the Uke's body; this lets me wrap my arm around their neck from the first point of contact (my shoulder) to the last point (my forearm). If done right Uke should tap from this alone. Then apply the other arm as before

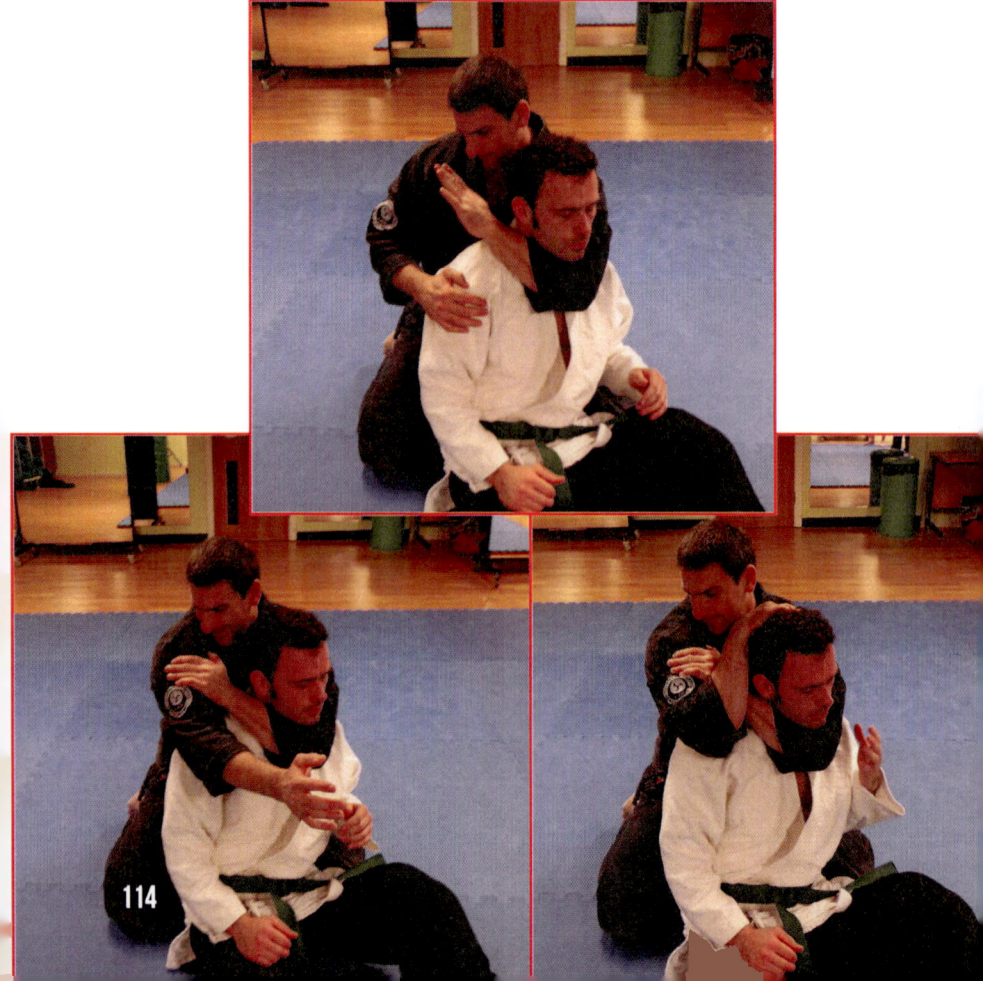

ATAMA HISHIGI
HEAD/FACE CRUSH

This is exactly the same principle as the other Hadaka Jimes. The only difference is that your forearm is across Uke's eye or jaw. It is very painful and although it is not as dangerous as the strangle or choke, still be careful when applying as the jaw can be easily dislocated or even fractured.

KUBI GARAMI
NECK LOCK

Again the same hand positioning as before but this time we are applying it side-on to Uke so that your chest is touching Uke's shoulder. Place your forearm to the side of Uke's neck and finish the technique in the same way as before, making sure that the hand on Uke's head is pushing is the head against your forearm.

If Uke starts to strike back you can always lift them up. They will stop and probably try to hold onto your arms.

Once again the same hand positioning but this time you are facing Uke. I use this technique a lot. It gives you plenty of control as well as the chance to strike to the head. Once in the body-cross position place one arm behind Uke's neck as this gives you a chance to strike with the other hand until you decide to finish Uke off. Grab your bicep as before and place your hand on to Uke's forehead; then place your feet under their legs and stretch out making sure you keep your legs wide apart and your whole body weight is on them.

CHOKES & STRANGLES

Instead of putting your hand onto Uke's forehead you can cause a bit more discomfort by pushing down with your knife-hand onto their jaw, upper lip, nose or eyes. Keep your hand at an angle (not flat across the mouth) to prevent Uke from biting you.

When applying **Hadaka Jime** from the standing position, break Uke's posture to stop them throwing your over their shoulder. To do this you can either push on the small of their back or hip with the palm of your hand, or knee them in the Coxis. You are looking to set up the strangle and have Uke's back arched so that you are keeping them up. To apply it, force Uke straight down to the floor to crumple them up. They should tap on the way down.

Do not walk backwards with them: you can't see behind you and might trip over. It also lays Uke out and stops the pressure on their spine.

CHOKES & STRANGLES

Also if you bring Uke straight down you can go down on one knee and drop their spine on it.

If you look at the 2nd picture once Uke has hit my knee he has let go of my arm to protect his back or to put his hand down to the ground. Also notice Uke's position with their heels up, back bent and neck pushed forward.

KOTE JIME
FOREARM STRANGLE

From the last technique you can put a strangle on just by moving your forearm across Uke's neck and grabbing your Gi sleeve. Try and grab the sleeve as close to your elbow as possible without lifting your body up too high and then focus on that elbow touching the ground.

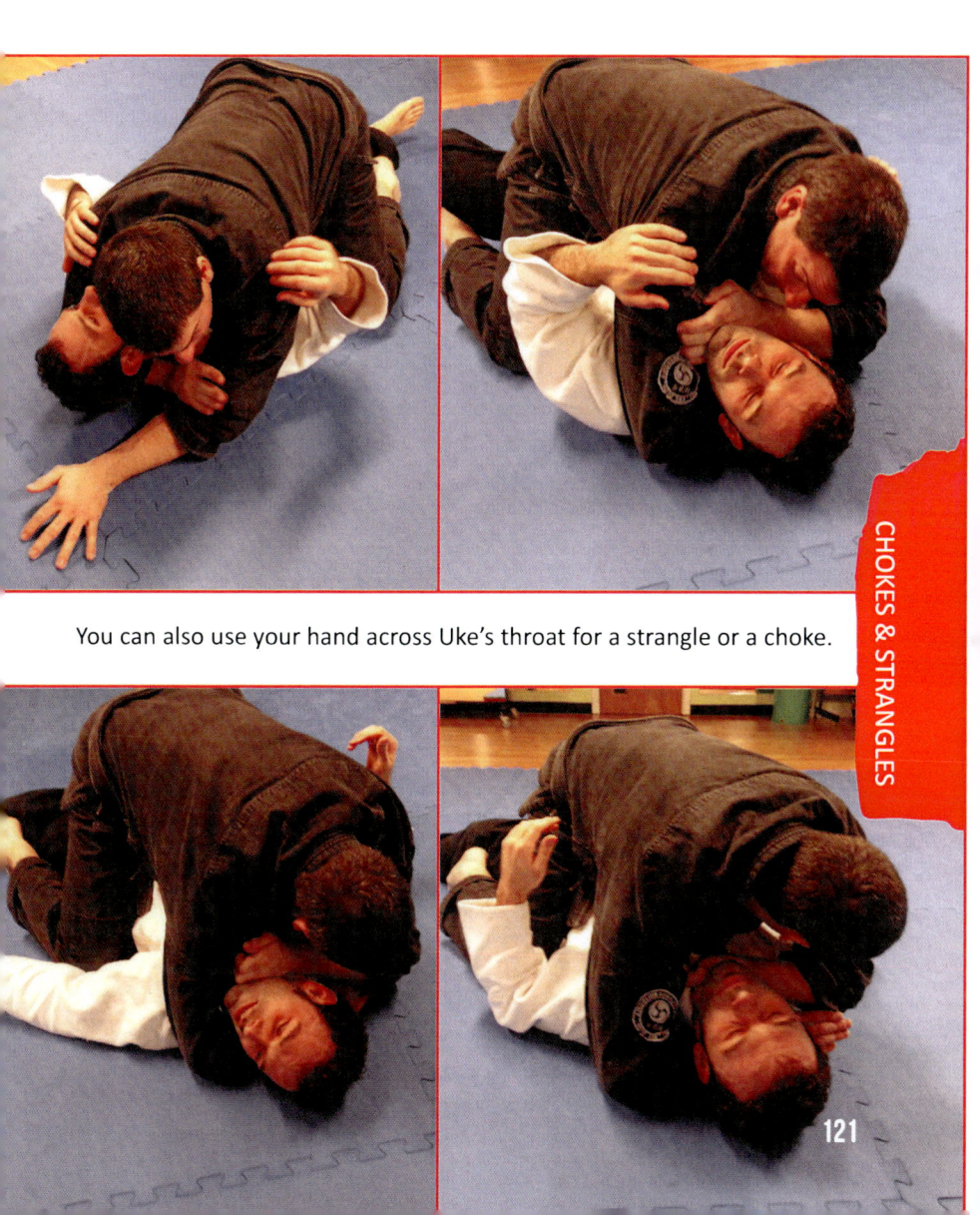

You can also use your hand across Uke's throat for a strangle or a choke.

CHOKES & STRANGLES

SODE GURUMA JIME
SLEEVE WHEEL

This technique is similar to the last one, but this time by grabbing your own sleeve you can put added pressure on the neck. Still focus on pushing your elbow to the floor. The first picture shows Tori holding onto the sleeve and forcing the knuckle from his little finger into the side of Uke's neck, aiming for the carotid archery.

The second picture shows the arm coming further around so that the forearm is more on Uke's throat, again changing it from a strangle to a choke.

KOTE JIME
FOREARM CHOKE

A nice and easy choke. Basically, place your forearm (blade of the arm) across Uke's throat and either push down or turn your wrist to push Uke's Adams apple up. Your other hand can cover one of Uke's arm; the other arm you trap with your leg.

MAE OKURI-ERI-JIME
FRONT SLIDING COLLAR

With this strangle it's best to grab Uke's lapel nice and high around the neck and concentrate on pushing your elbow to the floor whilst pulling the lapel the other side down towards their opposite hip. Keep your weight on Uke and make sure their back is flat on the floor.

USHIRO-OKURI-ERI-JIME
SLIDING COLLAR FROM THE BACK

This uses the same principle as the last technique, but this time it is done from behind Uke. As before, grab Uke's lapel high on the neck with one hand, and with the other hand grab the other lapel about chest height. With the top hand focus on bringing your elbow back; with the bottom hand pull the lapel towards Uke's opposite hip. You must keep your chest tight to Uke's back so that there is no movement between you..

CHOKES & STRANGLES

If Uke tries to grab your arm to prevent the strangle, take advantage of this by grabbing their arm just above the elbow, then pulling it across their body and pulling your top elbow back as before.

ROLLING OKURI ERI JIME

With Uke on all fours you need to pass your hand under their throat and take hold of their lapel. Step your leg over them to place the foot next to their knee. Notice that your other hand comes behind Uke's leg to catch it during the roll.

CHOKES & STRANGLES

Once you have rolled Uke over you have a few options: you can hold Uke's leg and their lapel and pull apart (fig 1) or bring their leg and head together, but keeping the strangling elbow high (fig 2) You can also let go of Uke's leg

FIG 1

FIG 2

and pull their arm back for a Ju Ji Jime, keeping the strangle on, and the leg over their waist to control them.

OKURI-ERI-JIME
SLIDING COLLAR ARM UNDER UKE'S

The version is very similar to the first one but the hand pulling the collar goes under Uke's arm. This helps in a couple of ways. If you had already got the hand around their throat and Uke realises what you are trying to achieve, Uke might bring their hand up to their head to block the strangle. In that case, all you need to do is go underneath their arm.

The second way it helps is that it stops Uke from rolling out and away from you.

Remember to keep your head in close to Uke's shoulder in case they try to elbow you.

CHOKES & STRANGLES

KATA-HA-JIME
SINGLE WING CHOKE

Another way of applying this technique is to let go of the collar with your bottom hand and place it behind Uke's head. You can put your palm on it or use the blade of your hand to place pressure onto the back of their neck.

NAMI JUJI JIME
CROSS STRANGLE – NORMAL VERSION

Nami-Juji-Jime is done by crossing your hands and sliding the fingers inside Uke's collar as high up and as tight as possible. The strangle is executed by either twisting both knuckles into Uke's carotid artery or jugular vein (at the side of their neck) or by pushing your elbows down to the floor.

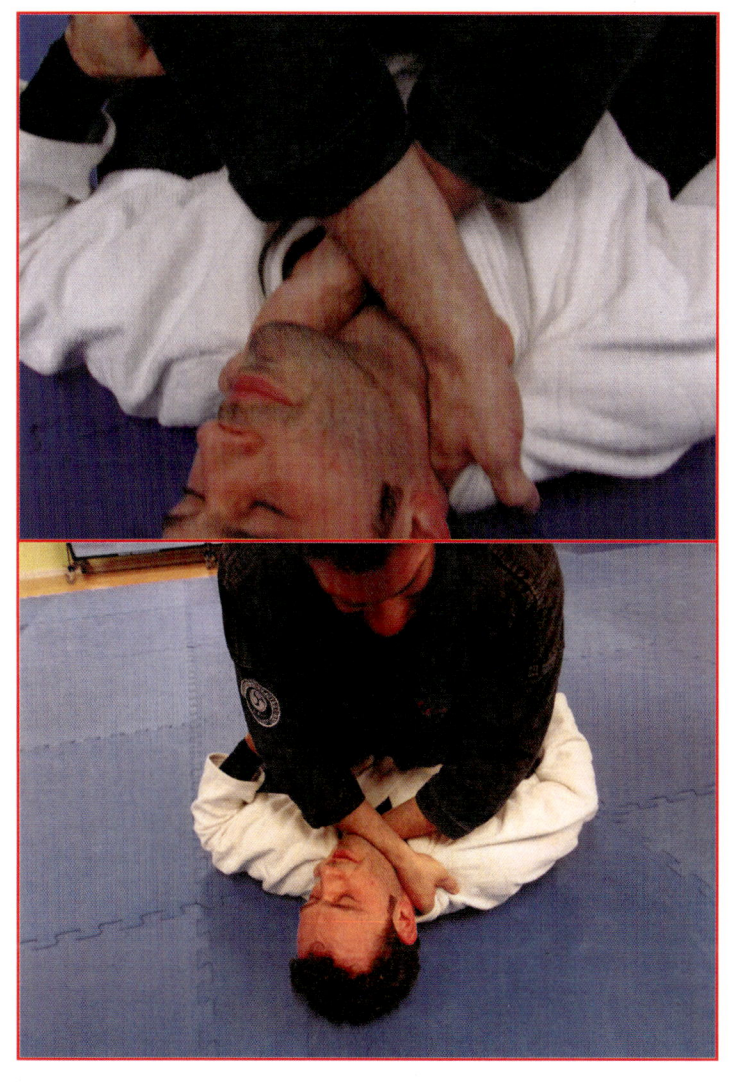

CHOKES & STRANGLES

NAMI JUJI JIME
CROSS STRANGLE WITH YOUR BACK ON THE FLOOR

If Uke is on top you can still do exactly the same technique either using your knuckles or pulling your elbows out to the side and your hands inwards to your chest.

GYAKU JUJI JIME
CROSS-STRANGLE – REVERSE

Using the same principles as the last strangle, this time both of your thumbs are inside Uke's collar. Finish the technique in the same way.

CHOKES & STRANGLES

KATA JUJI JIME
CROSS-STRANGLE – HALF

The same strangle again, but this time one thumb on one hand is inside the collar and the other hand the fingers are inside Ukes collar. Finish in the same way.

With any of the previous four techniques if Uke tucks in their chin so as to stop you putting the strangle on, then simply carry on with the technique but place your forearm across their jaw or eye socket and finish as before.

Another version from the cross-strangle repertoire is we grab Uke's collar with both hands and leave one hand slightly lower. This gives us a dominant hand which will put the strangle on, or if moved across to Uke's throat, change it to a choke. Focus mainly on the forearm doing the work and just keeping tension on with the other hand.

CHOKES & STRANGLES

USHIRO NAMI JUJI JIME

The last of the cross-strangles: this time we are behind Uke with our chest to their back. This technique requires your thumbs inside Uke's collar (unless you have really flexible wrists). You will need to bend your wrists slightly to get your thumb knuckle tight into the side of Uke's neck. Once both of your thumbs are in position grab the collars tightly and pull your elbows back so that they are higher than your shoulders. Keep on pulling until Uke taps.

TE ASHI JIME
HAND FOOT STRANGLE

This technique is very similar to Ashi Jime (page 149) except the foot and hand swap places. In this technique the foot is behind Uke's neck and the arm comes across the throat.

The first thing to do is to get your leg across the back of Uke's neck and grab it with your opposite hand, then pull them onto you. Then, with your other hand, grab either Uke's lapel or your own forearm and pull your leg down and push the strangling arm's elbow up.

CHOKES & STRANGLES

SANKUKA JIME
TRIANGLE STRANGLE

This is used frequently in ring/caged sports because it is very hard to escape from and, as with other strangles used in these sports, it gives Uke plenty of time to tap before serious damage is done. There are many different ways to apply this technique but here I will try to simplify it and give you a few options. First take control of Uke's wrist then bring the leg on the opposite side of your body across the back of Uke's neck, then bring your other leg up straight and bend it, trapping your own ankle.

You can always hold your own ankle, pulling it down to make sure that it is tight across Uke's neck. Once you have Uke's head locked in, move their arm across your body and so that it is tight across their throat. To finish the technique bring your leg down tight and pull your thighs into your chest. If Uke is not tapping yet, place your hands on the back of their head and pull down. If your legs are not that flexible you might find it easier to pull your body round 90 degrees to Uke.

STRAIGHT ON

AT 90 DEGREES

CHOKES & STRANGLES

YOKO SANKUKA JIME
SIDE TRIANGLE STRANGLE

Uke has got you held down in Yoko Shiho Gatame, so for this technique we need to get Uke's head up. We can do this by either putting your thumb under their jaw bone and pushing up, or in the hole just under their ear.

Once Uke's head is up high enough, bring your leg over their head and pull down to trap your foot under your other leg; then squeeze both legs down to the floor.

Keep Uke's arm trapped

CHOKES & STRANGLES

141

USHIRO SANKUKA JIME
BACK TRIANGLE STRANGLE

This technique works well when you have tried to get Uke in a rear strangle but they have managed to wriggle down and out of it.

Once Uke gets low enough bring your leg across their throat and your other leg over your foot. Then bend your leg to put the strangle on. It doesn't matter if Uke has an arm trapped or not, the strangle will still work.

UDE GARAMI JIME
ENTANGLED STRANGLE

To start you'll need to take control of Uke's opposite wrist by grabbing it when they are punching or trying to grab you. Once you have control of Uke's wrist you need to force it across their face and plant their hand on the floor. Bring your other hand under Uke's neck and grab the wrist that you have planted. Keep your weight on and their arm tight across their face.

Now release Uke's arm slightly and slide your other hand under Uke's arm and grab your own wrist; now pull everything tight again.

CHOKES & STRANGLES

You could also leave your hand open and wedge it under Uke's jaw line, when the technique there, it will put a lot of pressure on the jaw and could facture or dislocate it.

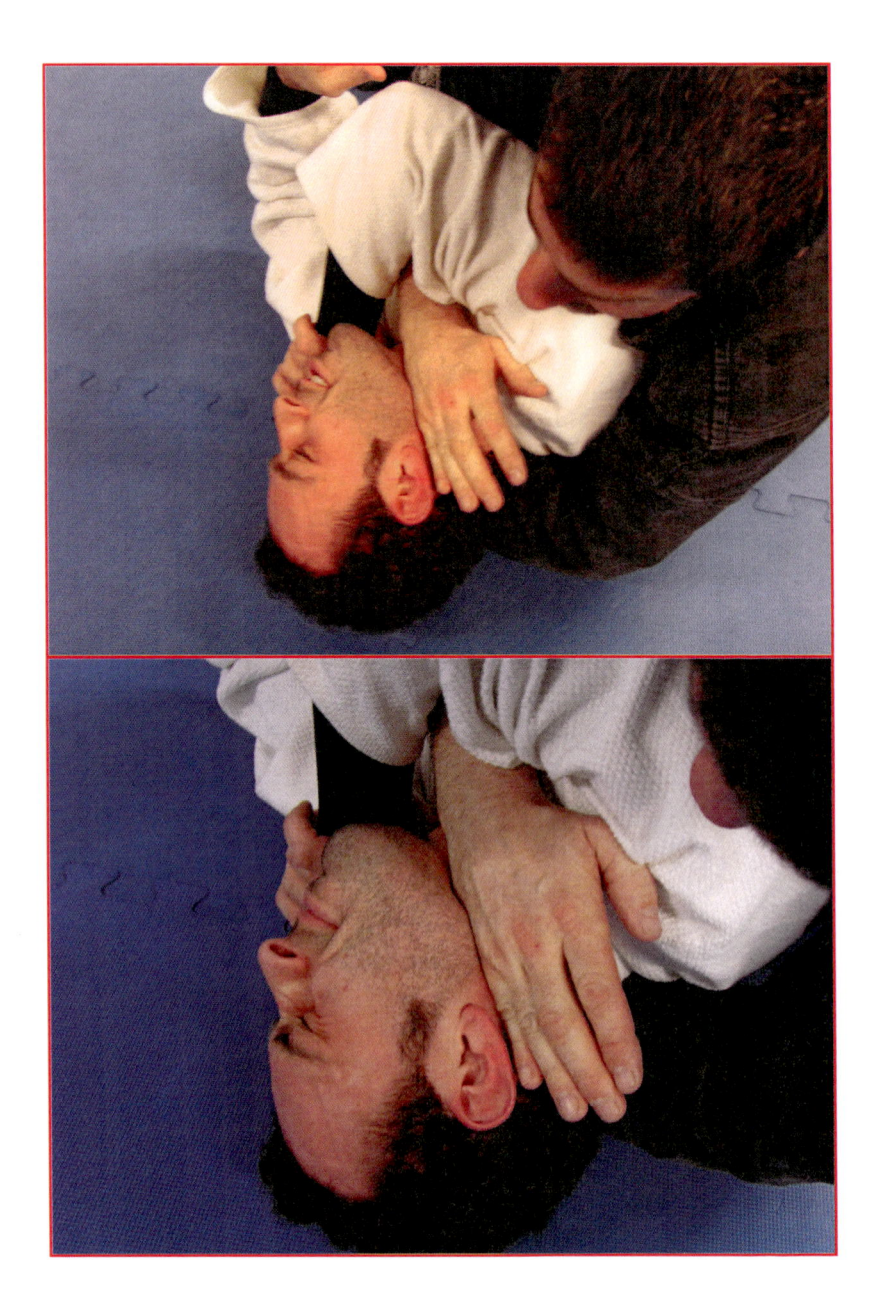

KATA GATAME JIME
SHOULDER-HOLD STRANGLE

With this technique you need to make sure that Uke's arm is tight across their neck. This can be done from Kata Gatami or Kesa Gatami. If you let go of the arm you are holding, Uke will try to escape by rolling away from your body. Let their arm go past your face and across their neck, then trap it by pushing your neck/head onto their tricep.

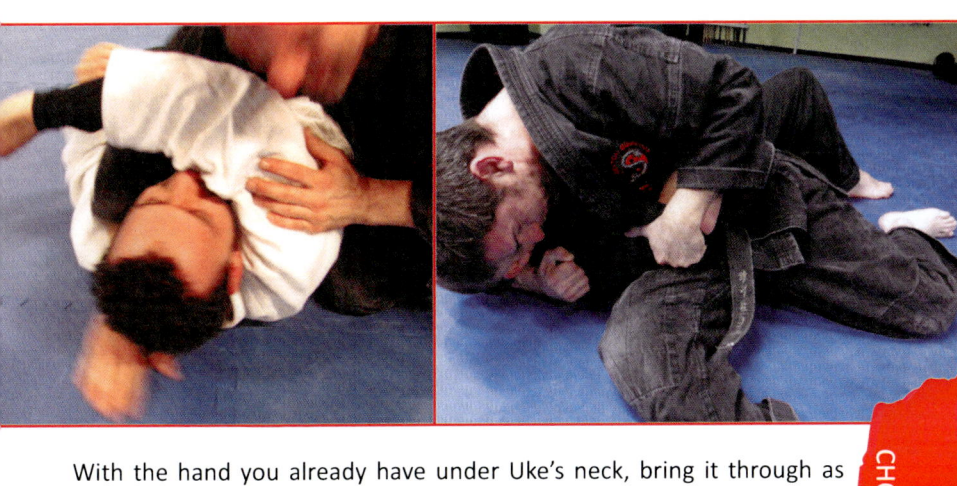

With the hand you already have under Uke's neck, bring it through as much as you can and hold onto your other forearm.

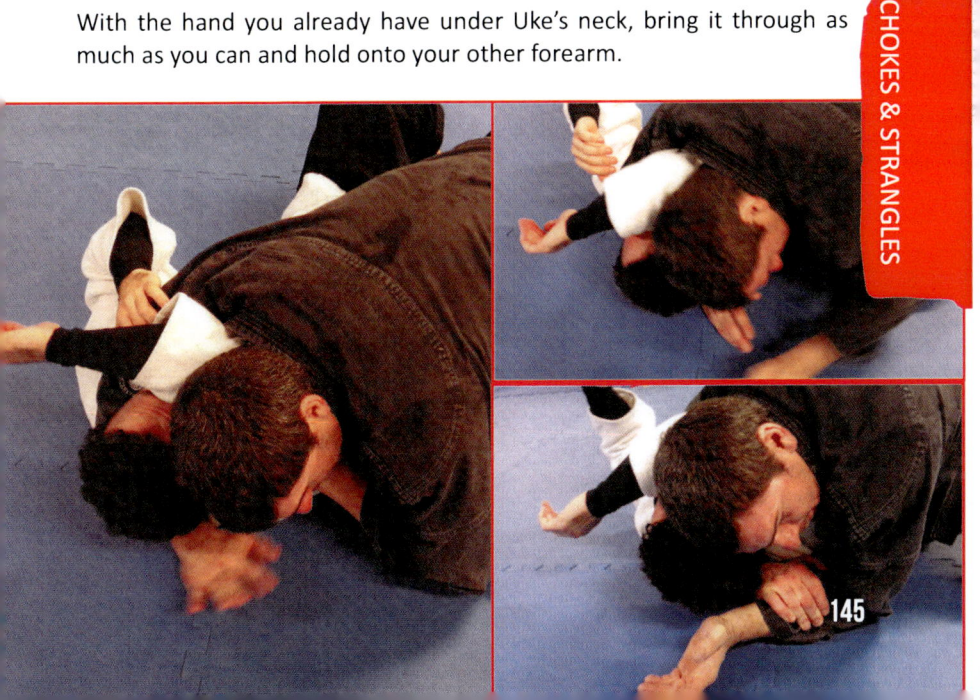

CHOKES & STRANGLES

Squeeze both arms in tight and take a deep breath in to expand your chest, keep the pressure on by pushing your head against Uke's arm.

Also if you bring both of your knees up as much as you can as if you are kneeling next to Uke, this will help to push your body weight down onto Uke's arm and head. With all of your weight in a small area it is extremely hard for Uke to move you in any direction.

TSUKI KOMI JIME
THRUSTING GI CHOKE

It is exactly what it says: thrusting their Gi to choke them. With Uke on their back, grab their opposite lapel about where their sternum is. Then grab the other side in the same place but pull it so that their Gi is loose enough to push across Uke's throat.

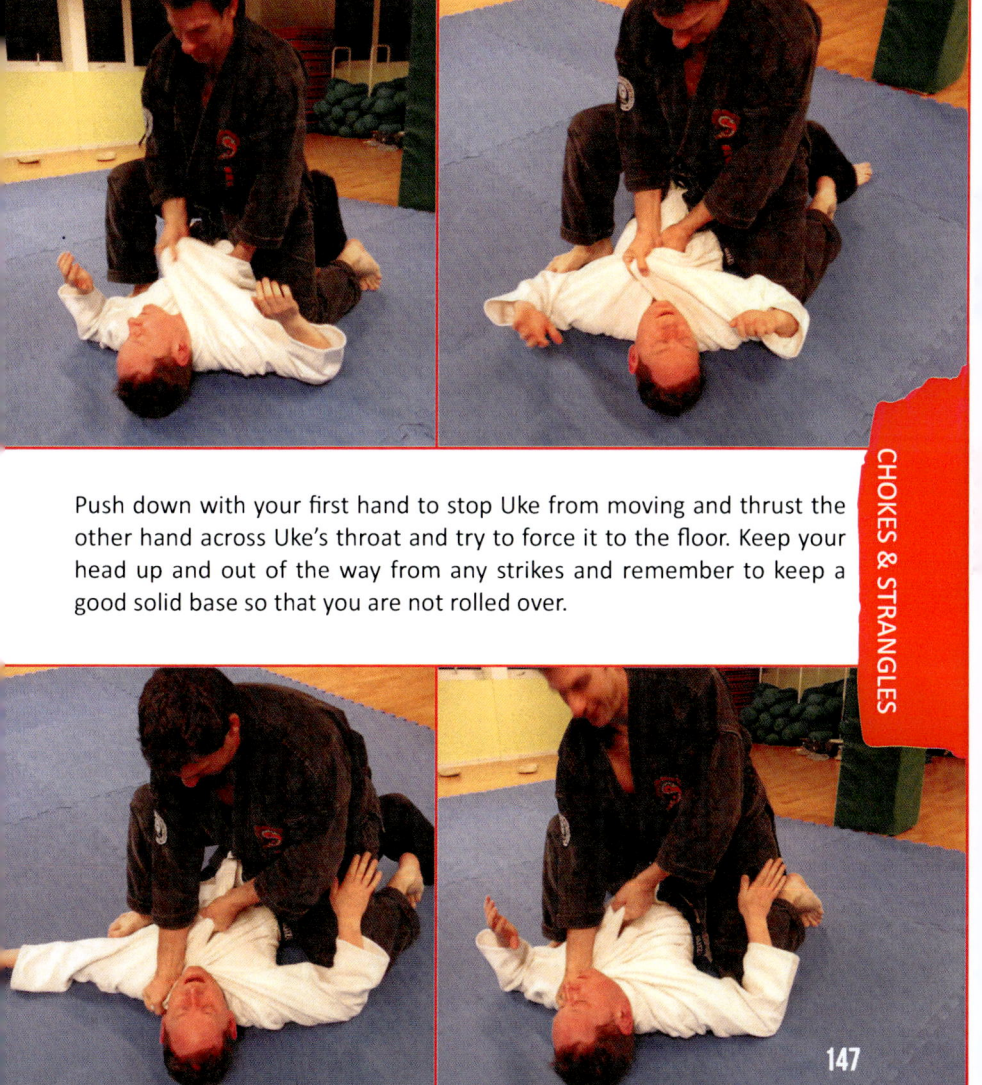

Push down with your first hand to stop Uke from moving and thrust the other hand across Uke's throat and try to force it to the floor. Keep your head up and out of the way from any strikes and remember to keep a good solid base so that you are not rolled over.

CHOKES & STRANGLES

KAITEN JIME
ROLLING STRANGLE

With Uke on all fours you'll need to grab their opposite lapel high and keep your forearm tight to their neck; then bring your other hand around their waist as you roll over them. The strangle will go on whilst you are rolling, so be carefull.

As you are rolling, trap Uke's arm and, when you are on your back, stretch their arm out. At the same time as this, pull your strangling arm back, but because your elbow is already on the floor you might need to slide your elbow up towards Uke's ear to finish the technique.

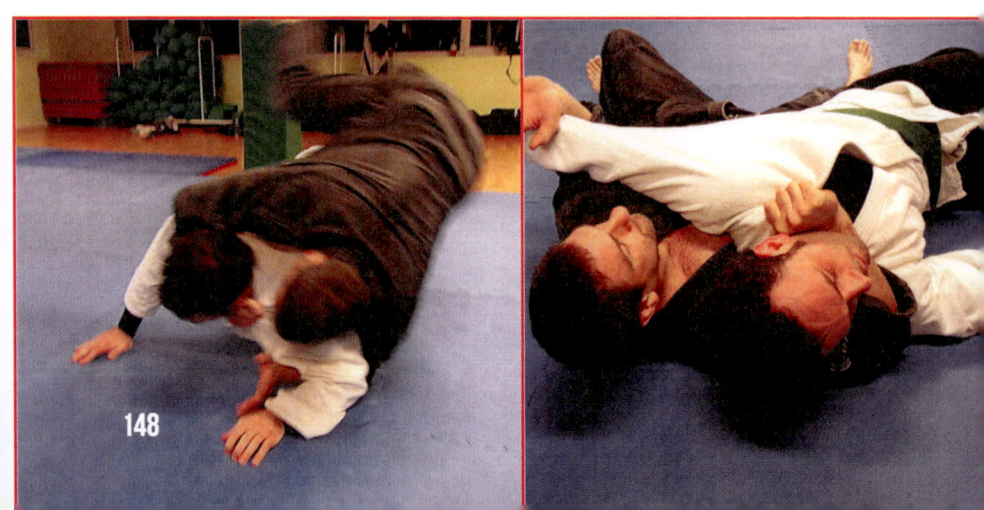

SHUTO JIME
KNIFE-HAND STRANGLE

Starting with the same position as the last strangle (Uke on all fours and you grabbing the opposite lapel), it is obvious that there is plenty of opportunity to strike Uke from here as well. Keeping the strangling hand tight to Uke's neck use the blade of your other forearm (hand open) to slowly slide across and down their neck to their windpipe, whilst at the same time pulling your other hand towards you.

CHOKES & STRANGLES

ASHI JIME
FOOT CHOKE

Ashi Jime is normally done when Tori is being pushed back or Uke is coming on to Tori with enough room for Tori to get his/her shin up and under Uke's throat. Once the foot is tucked in place you again have plenty of options: you can grab both of Uke's lapels and pull down onto your shin; you can hold onto your own foot and pull down; or you can pull on the back of Uke's head on to your shin.

OBI JIME
BELT STRANGLE

Again, this is exactly as it sounds. With Uke laying on their side or their front simply pass your belt around their neck and pull tight. If Uke has their chin tucked in then just wrap the belt under the nose and pull back.

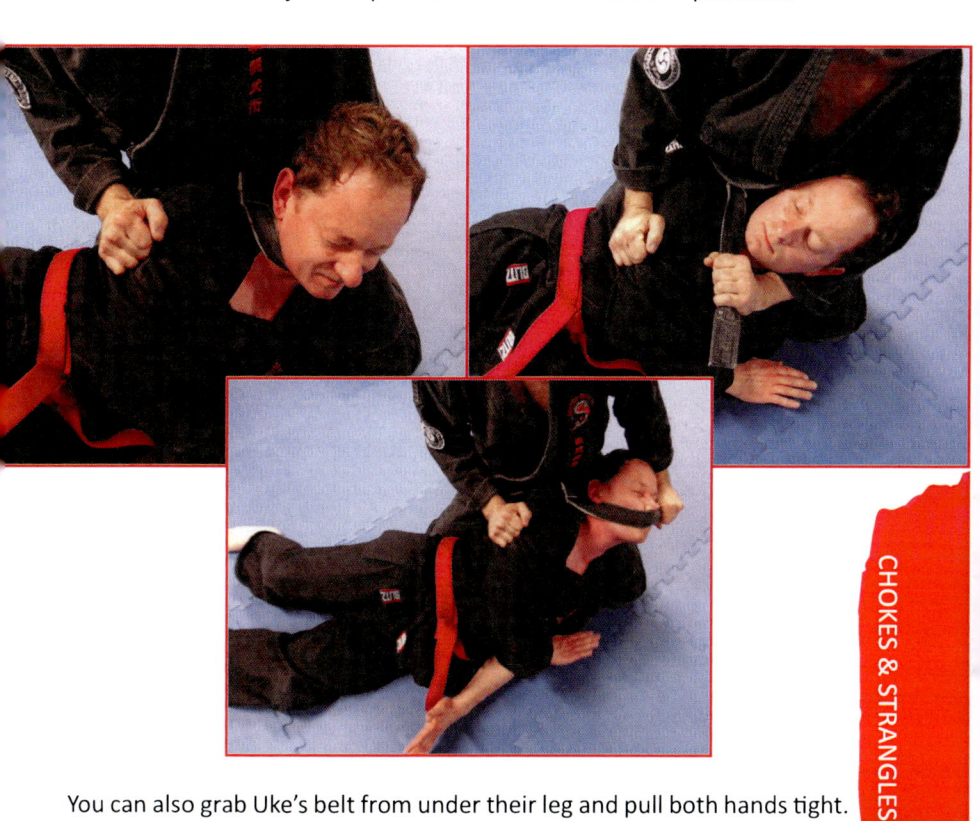

You can also grab Uke's belt from under their leg and pull both hands tight.

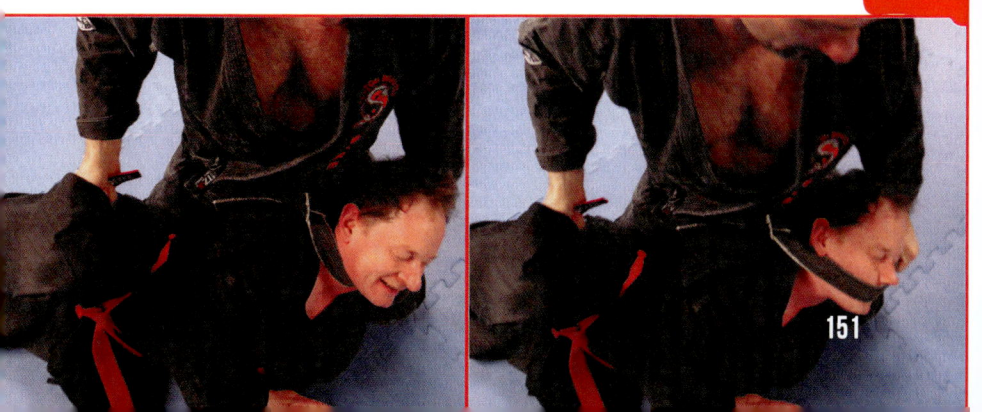

You can use a hoodie in the same way. It's possible to grab the top of the hood and wrap it around Uke's neck. It doesn't matter which way you wrap it.

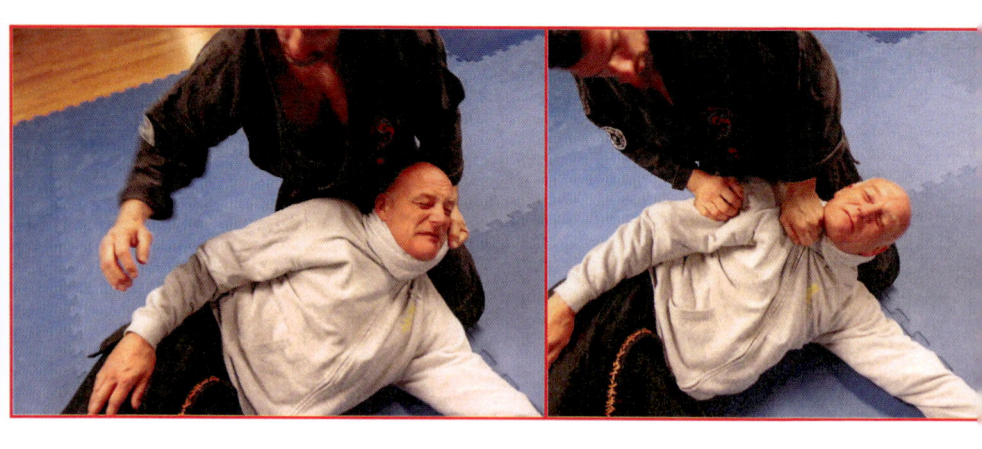

Also you can leave the hood up and pull it partially across Uke's face and pull and twist.

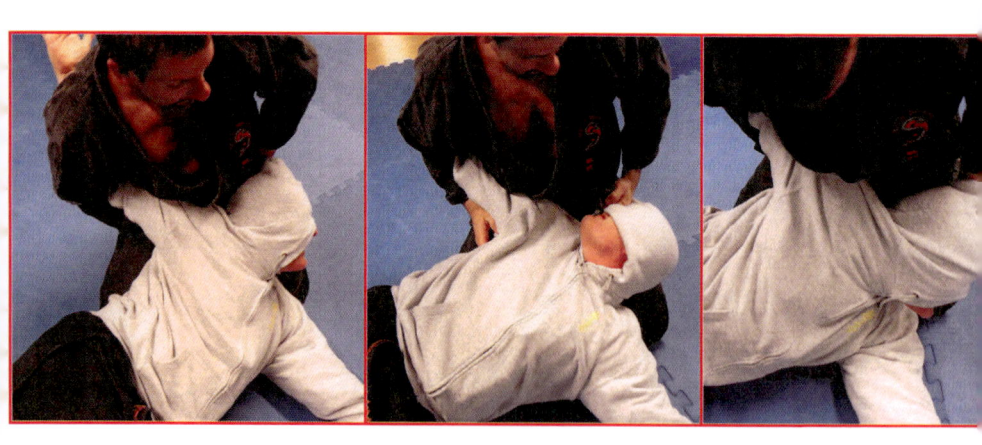

No hood either then use their own hair if they have enough.

152

KOTE GURUMA JIME
LOOP CHOKE

To apply this choke you need to grab Uke's opposite lapel with your thumb on the outside of their Gi. The blade of your forearm will go across Uke's throat and once you have Uke's lapel you now need to get their head down either by punching, using pressure points, or just by brute force. Then pass your other arm over the top of their head and either grab your opposite elbow, or wedge your hand under your opposite arm.

CHOKES & STRANGLES

NODO HISHIGI
THROAT CRUSH FROM TOMOE NAGE

This choke is done from Tomoe Nage (stomach/circle throw). Once you have thrown Uke and they are on their back you need to quickly pass one arm over their head, leaving their lapel over their throat. Then roll onto your front bringing your other hand on top of the first. Both hands should be over Uke's throat now, so twist them into their Adam's apple and push down.

JIGOKU JIME
HELL STRANGLE

You may ask when is anybody going to get on all fours in a real fight? Well, if they have been kicked in the stomach and winded, kicked in the groin, thrown or slipped, that's when and to stop you from kicking them or to try and take you down, they will go for your legs.

Hell strangle also starts with Uke on all fours. Wrap your legs around an arm and bend over them to grab their other arm. Then roll backwards onto your side (this will keep Uke's neck bent forward) keep control of their arm with one hand and grab their furthest lapel with your other hand and pull. You should now have both arms trapped and the strangle on, so be aware that Uke may not be able to tap with their hands.

CHOKES & STRANGLES

You can also release your legs and bring your top leg over Uke's head, this applies more pressure to the strangle and to their neck.

Or if you grab Uke's other lapel you can use your thumb (Keito) to push into their vein, artery or throat.

MAE HADAKA JIME
FRONT NAKED CHOKE

From facing Uke use a back elbow/forearm strike to the side of their head then circle your arm around their neck until the blade of your forearm is on Uke's throat. Then either join your hands together and lift up or grab your own Gi lapel as high as you can and straighten your back. You can obviously elbow strike to the spine or neck if you like, or if you need more control, fall backwards (keeping the choke on) and then cross your legs around Uke before straightening your body out.

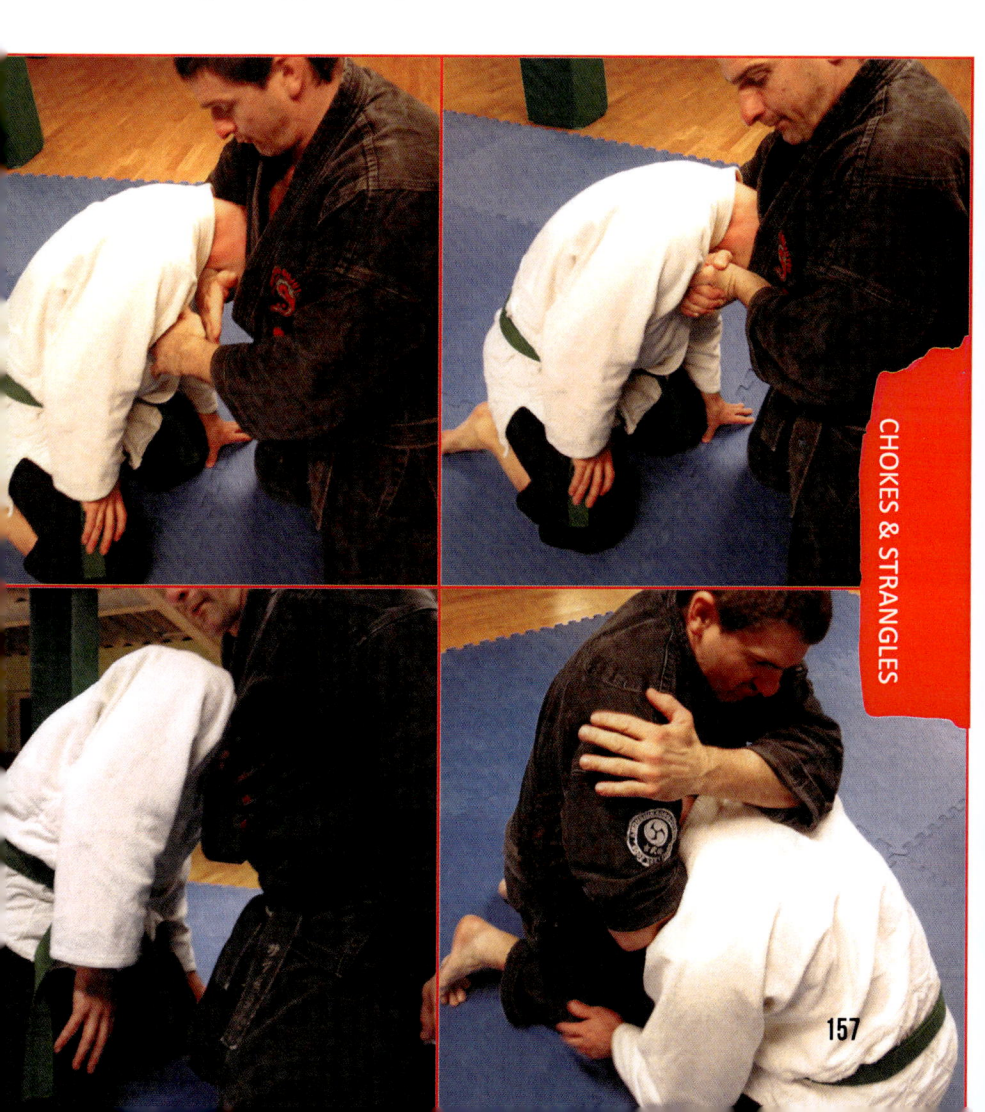

CHOKES & STRANGLES

KUBI GATAMI
NECK LOCKS

Now we are looking at the neck locks. As before be very careful with these; they can be extremely dangerous and a broken neck could mean paralysis.

The last choke leads us nicely into neck locks. Following the same principle as in that choke, this time catch Uke's chin with your forearm and force their head to the side (keep Uke's head trapped under your armpit as it can come out quite easy). Then again, either join your hands or this time hold on to your bicep.

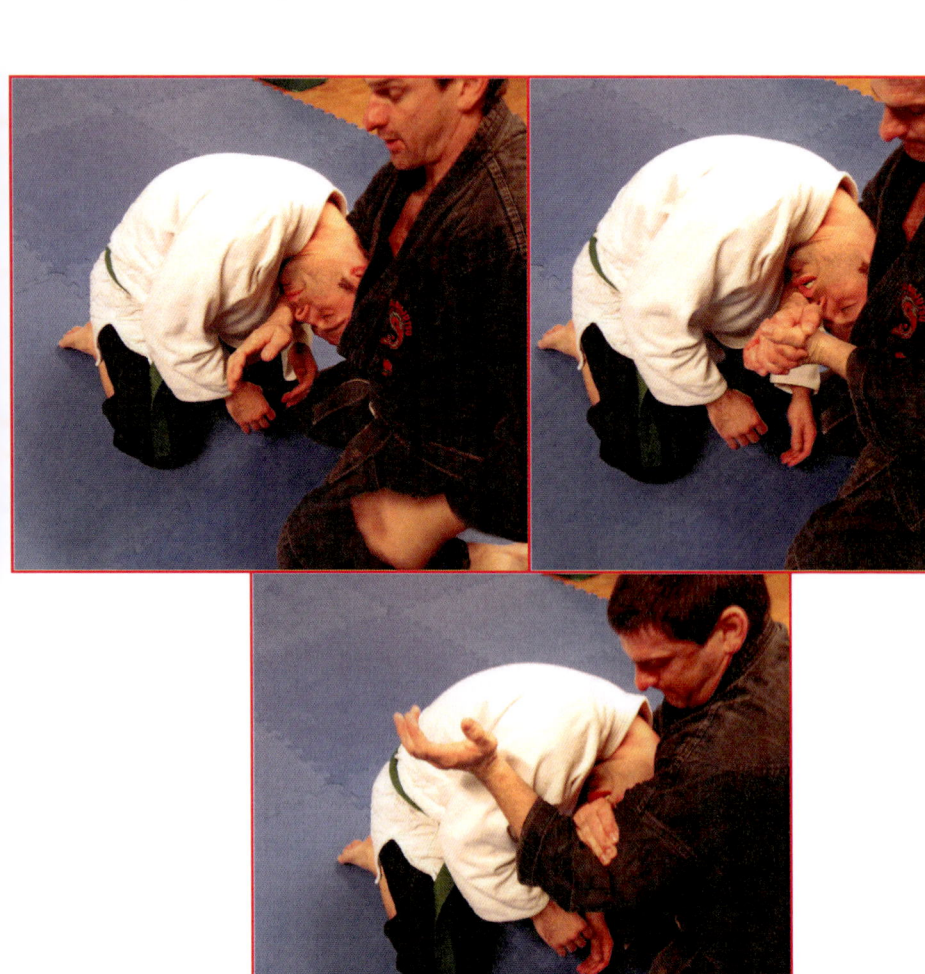

YOKO KUDI GATAMI
SIDE NECK LOCK

This time Uke is on their side. You should have your knees apart but touching their back to stop them rolling back onto you. Push your arm past Uke's arm, behind their head and in front of their other arm. Now focus on placing your hand on the floor past their face and keep your arm bent until the hand is planted, then straighten your arm slowly. Keep your body weight on the hand as you straighten your arm. You have your other hand to strike with, just in case breaking their neck isn't enough for you...

CHOKES & STRANGLES

USHIRO KUBI GATAMI
BACK/REVERSE NECK LOCK

With this lock you are behind Uke and you need to get your arm around their head so that the blade of your forearm is on the back of Uke's neck. Join hands (monkey grip). Once you have them in this position you'll need to get on your knees and straighten your back. Uke will have to get up, too, otherwise their neck will break. In doing so, however, all their weight will still be on their neck.

This technique can also be done from standing and is even more uncomfortable for Uke, plus you can control them with just one hand so that you can strike, knee or kick them as well.

CHOKES & STRANGLES

If you look at all of the pictures, Uke is holding on trying to stop his weight pushing on his neck.

MAE HIKI KUBI GATAMI
FRONT PULLING NECK LOCK

A very simple lock. With Uke being held in Tate Shiho Gatame (body cross hold) grab the back of Uke's head near the top with both hands and pull in towards your chest. You will need to bring one leg up and out for stability. Don't force Uke's head too high otherwise they might be able to resist. Try and pull their chin onto their chest so that the whole top half of their back is curled up. From this position if Uke tries to punch you they won't be able to get enough power into the strike and with the twisting of the body it will hurt them even more.

NEJIRE KUBI GATAMI
TWISTING NECK LOCK

This is from the same position as the last lock, but this time instead of pulling Uke's head towards you, you'll need to lift it up and then slowly twist it to the side. If Uke is resisting you might find it easier to have your forearm along their face and use your elbow to push their chin/jaw. This will also give you more control.

USHIRO HIKI KUBI GATAMI
BACKWARDS PULLING NECK LOCK

Uke is lying on their front with Tori kneeling astride them. Pull Uke's head back as far as it will go, either straight back or twisted. If Uke resists you have a few choices. Push your elbow on their back to bring their head up; or put your fingers in either their eyes or nostrils, or put a finger under their nose. You could grab their chin, pull their ears, or fish hook or grab their cheek or top lip.

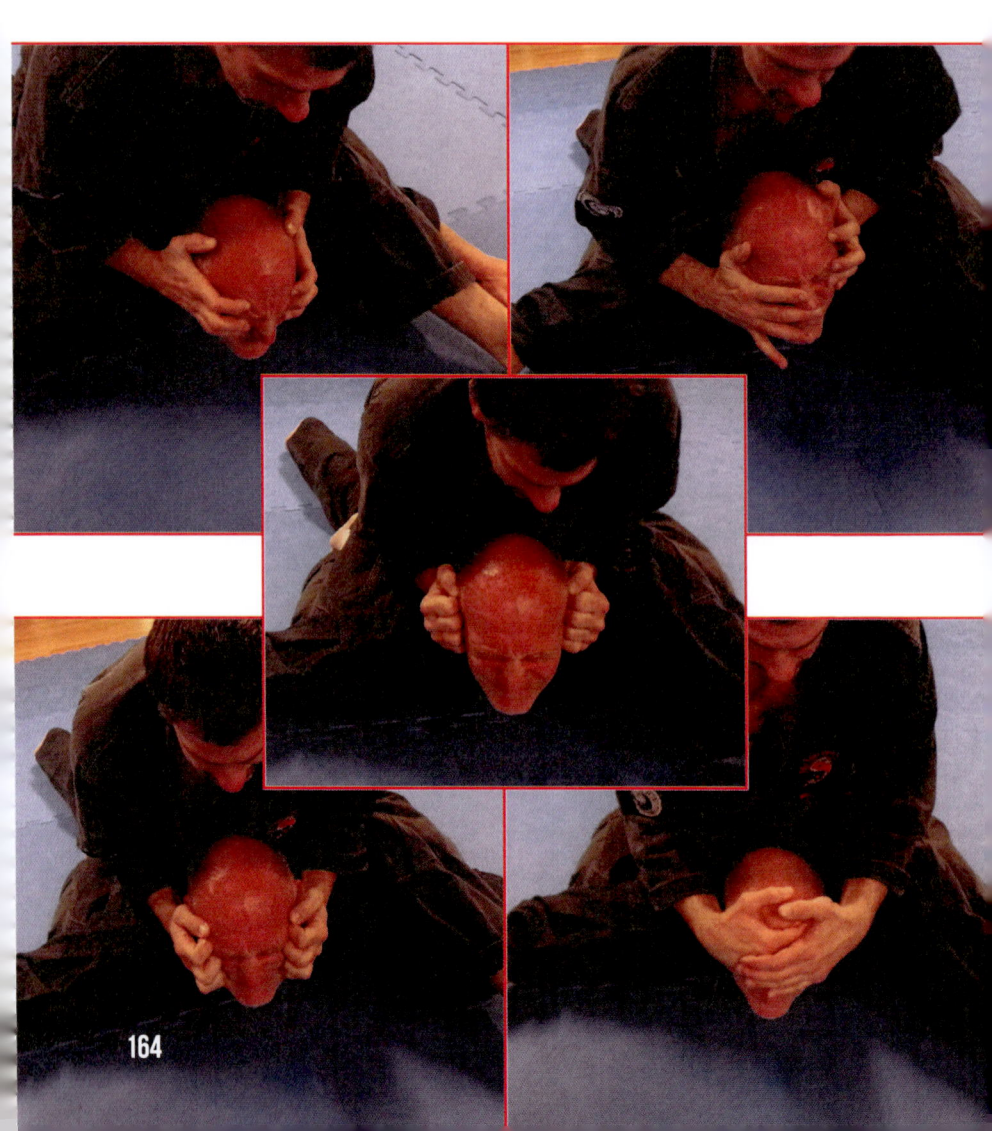

ADVANCED QUICK CHOKES

Advanced because they can cause a lot of damage very quickly, so these are not taught to beginners.

TE JIME
HAND CHOKE

Have your thumb bent as if in a "C" shape and put it on the side of Uke's windpipe. Now you can either put your fingers on the other side or on the hinge of their jaw to give them two lots of pain. Then just squeeze.

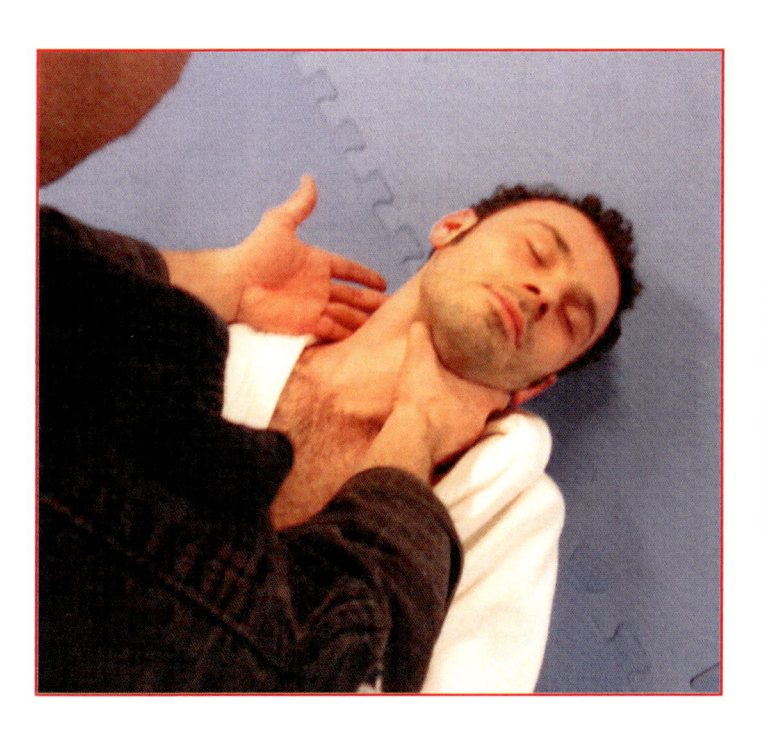

CHOKES & STRANGLES

This hand position (Toho) is also a great strike because you can use the web of the hand, thumb or fingers to strike the throat or face.

MOROTE TE JIME
DOUBLE-HAND CHOKE (INSIDE)

For this choke, place your thumbs into the side of Uke's windpipe and cross your thumbs over. Squeeze the windpipe, which is pulled in two directions, so when Uke tries to pull your wrist apart to stop the choke, they actually put it on harder.

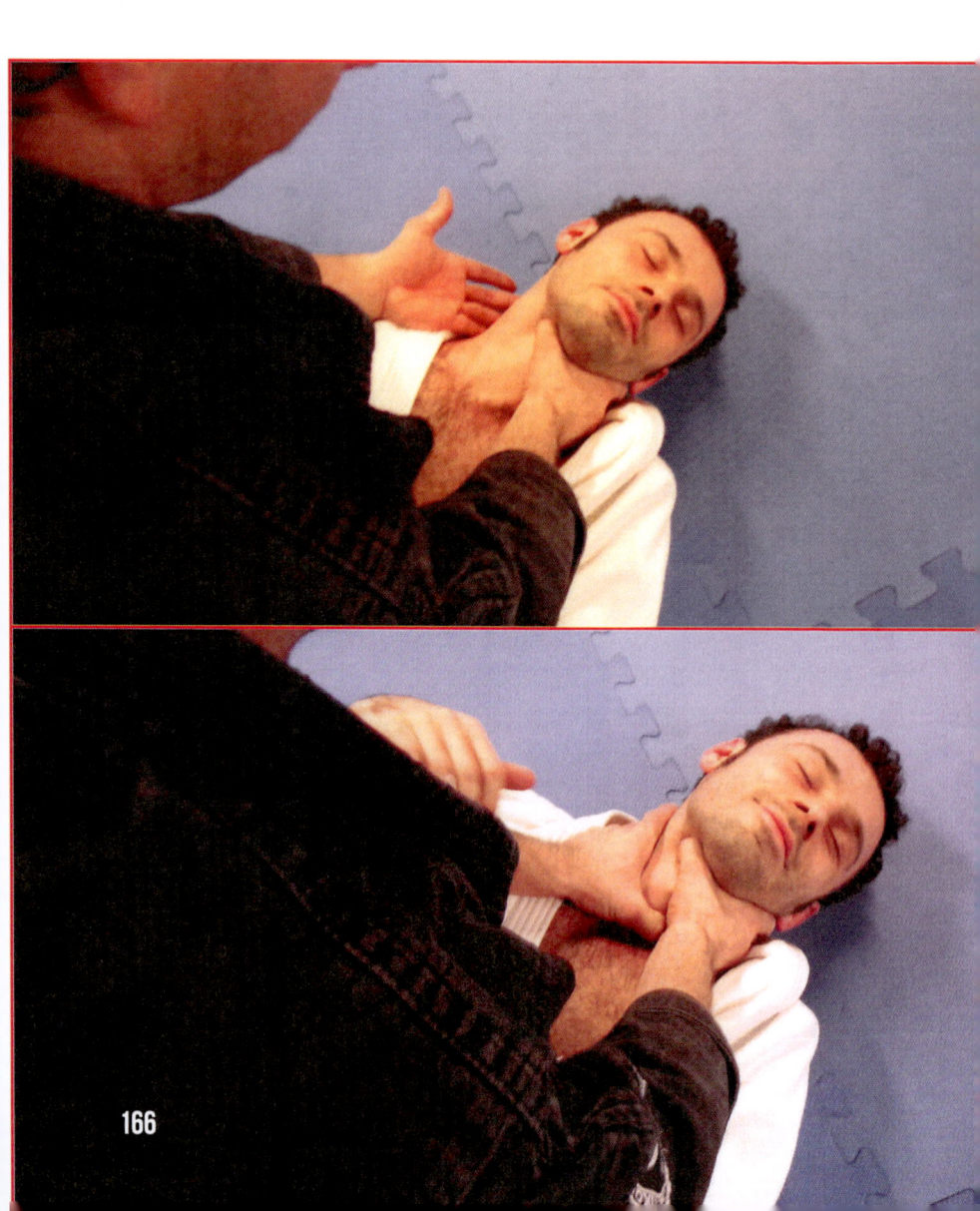

MOROTE TE JIME
DOUBLE-HAND CHOKE (OUTSIDE)

Working on the same principle as the last choke, this time the thumbs are on the outside of Uke's windpipe and you slowly try to make your thumbs meet (obviously Uke should tap long before this happens). With these techniques you can either trap Uke's arms with your knees or keep a slight bend in your arms so that you are keeping your distance and have time to block any strikes.

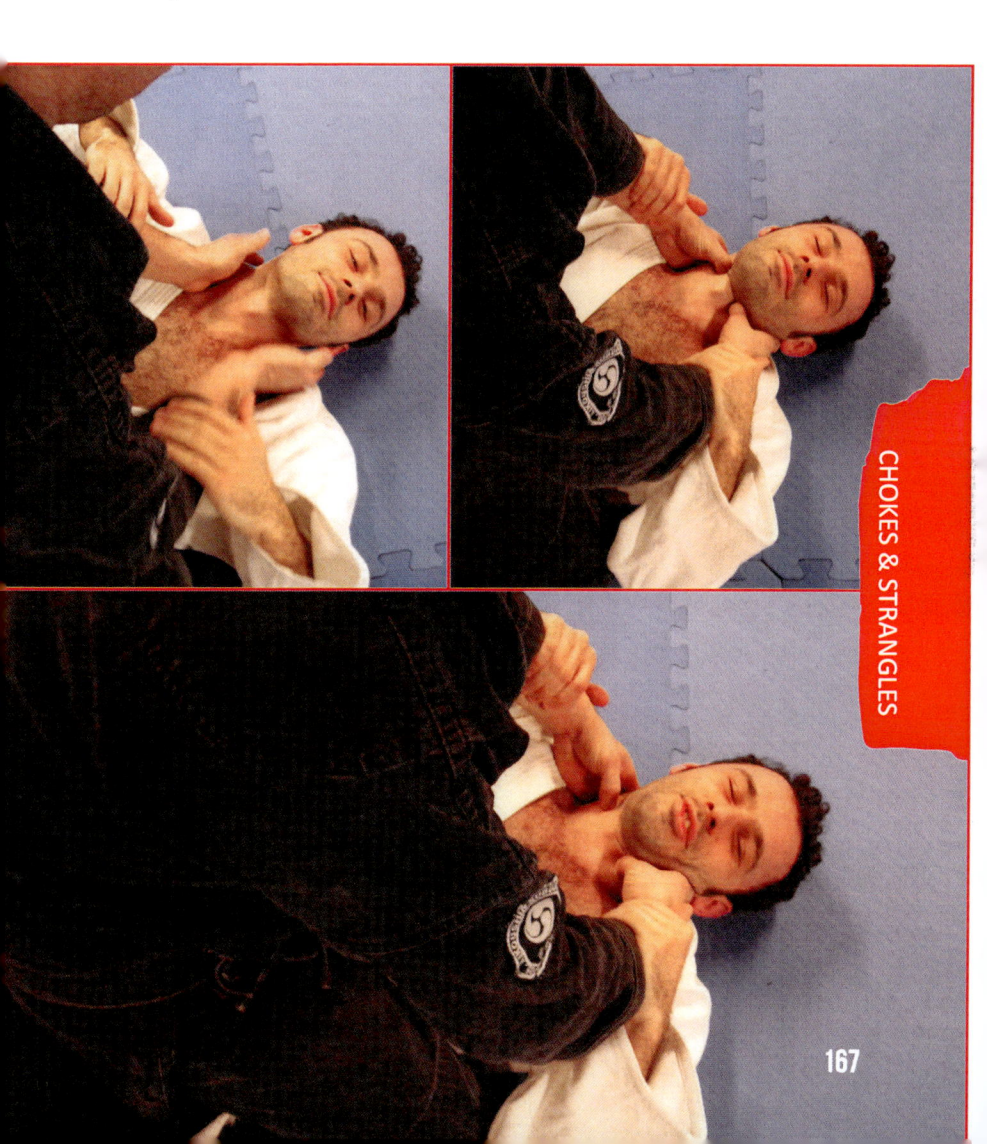

NUKITE JIME
FINGER CHOKE

For this choke, place your thumbs into the side of Uke's windpipe and cross your thumbs over. Squeeze the windpipe, which is pulled in two directions, so when Uke tries to pull your wrist apart to stop the choke, they actually put it on harder.

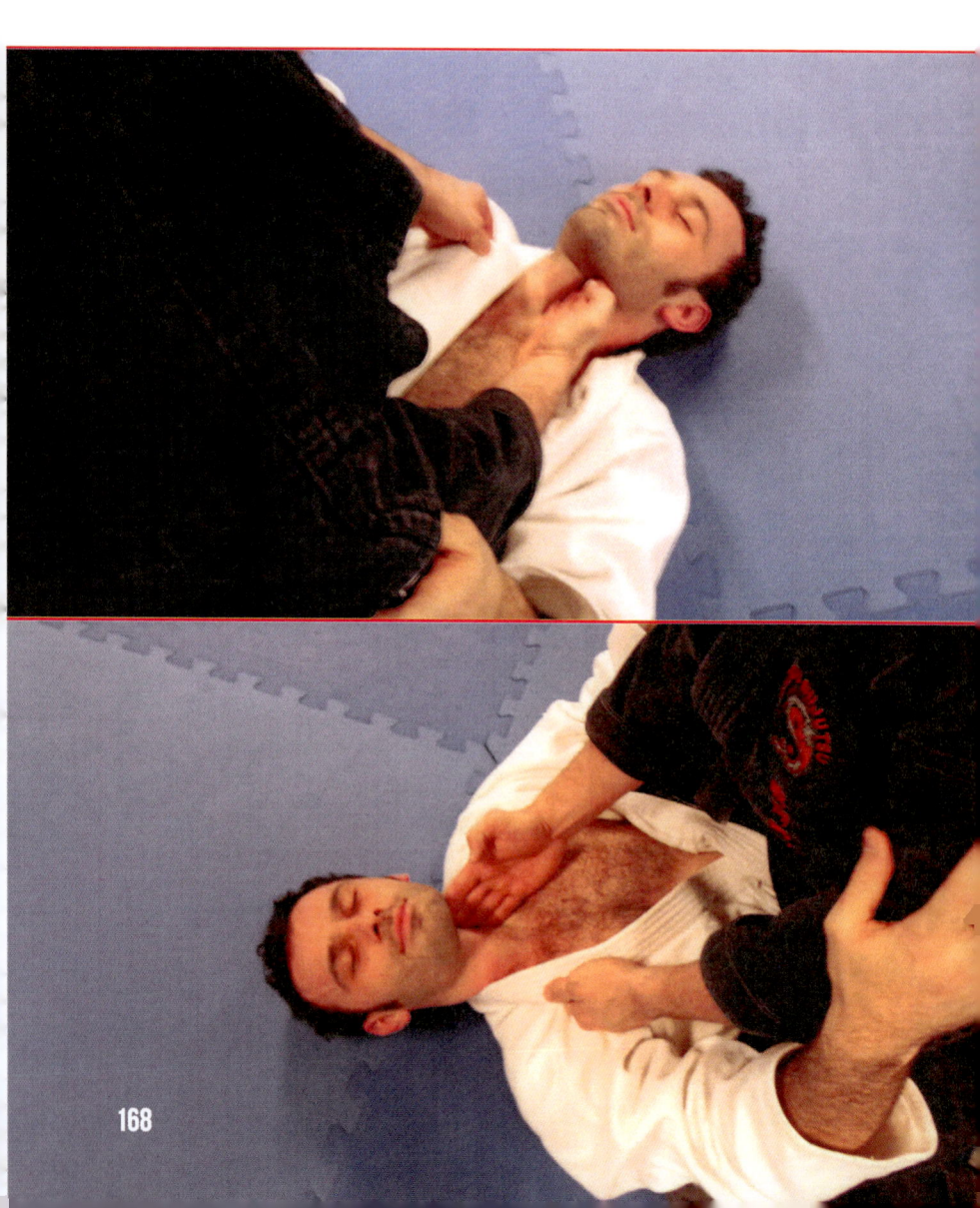

IPPON KEN
SINGLE KNUCKLE

This cheeky little technique causes a lot of pain. Grab hold of Uke's collars with your index fingers out and bent. You are using the middle knuckle of the index finger for the technique. For added strength to the finger, you should place your thumb tight against it. Roll your index-finger knuckles into the side of Uke's neck or throat. We are using leverage from the collars for more strength.

You can cause more pain by pushing into the jaw hinge, under the ear, chin bone... actually, anywhere on the face.

CHOKES & STRANGLES

ENPI
ELBOW

Extremely easy to apply and if Uke doesn't tap than they will surely move a lot to avoid it, which will create more opportunities for you. Place your elbow into the side of Uke's neck, jaw or throat, obviously you could strike with it as well.

MAE DO JIME
FRONT TRUNK STRANGLE

There are four basic ways to apply this strangle. The first sees you on your back and Uke between your legs. Wrap your legs around Uke's waist (not too high) and cross your feet behind their back. Straighten your legs and lift your hips up, thinking about your knees crushing Uke's floating ribs. You have good control with this technique and can pull Uke in or push them away with your legs.

CHOKES & STRANGLES

USHIRO DO JIME
BACK TRUNK STRANGLE

This works in the same principle as the last technique but you are behind Uke. Trap your legs around Uke's waist again, cross your feet, straighten your legs and lift your hips if possible.

Of course, striking to the spine, neck and head are all possibilities.

YOKO DO JIME
SIDE TRUNK STRANGLE

This time the legs are in a different position. Think of it more as a Sankuka Jime (triangle) leg position.

You have Uke side-on; bring one leg across their waist and bend it. Then bring the other leg over the top and squeeze down keeping everything tight. Use your foot/ankle to push onto Uke's floating rib and, if you can, take control of their arm to stop them rolling out.

CHOKES & STRANGLES

TE DO JIME
HAND TRUNK STRANGLE

Again this is best done side-on because it will give you the best angle and position to squeeze Uke's floating ribs. You are side-on to Uke, bring your arms around their waist and join your hands together using the monkey grip and pull in. Concentrate on the blade of your forearm cutting into the floating rib.

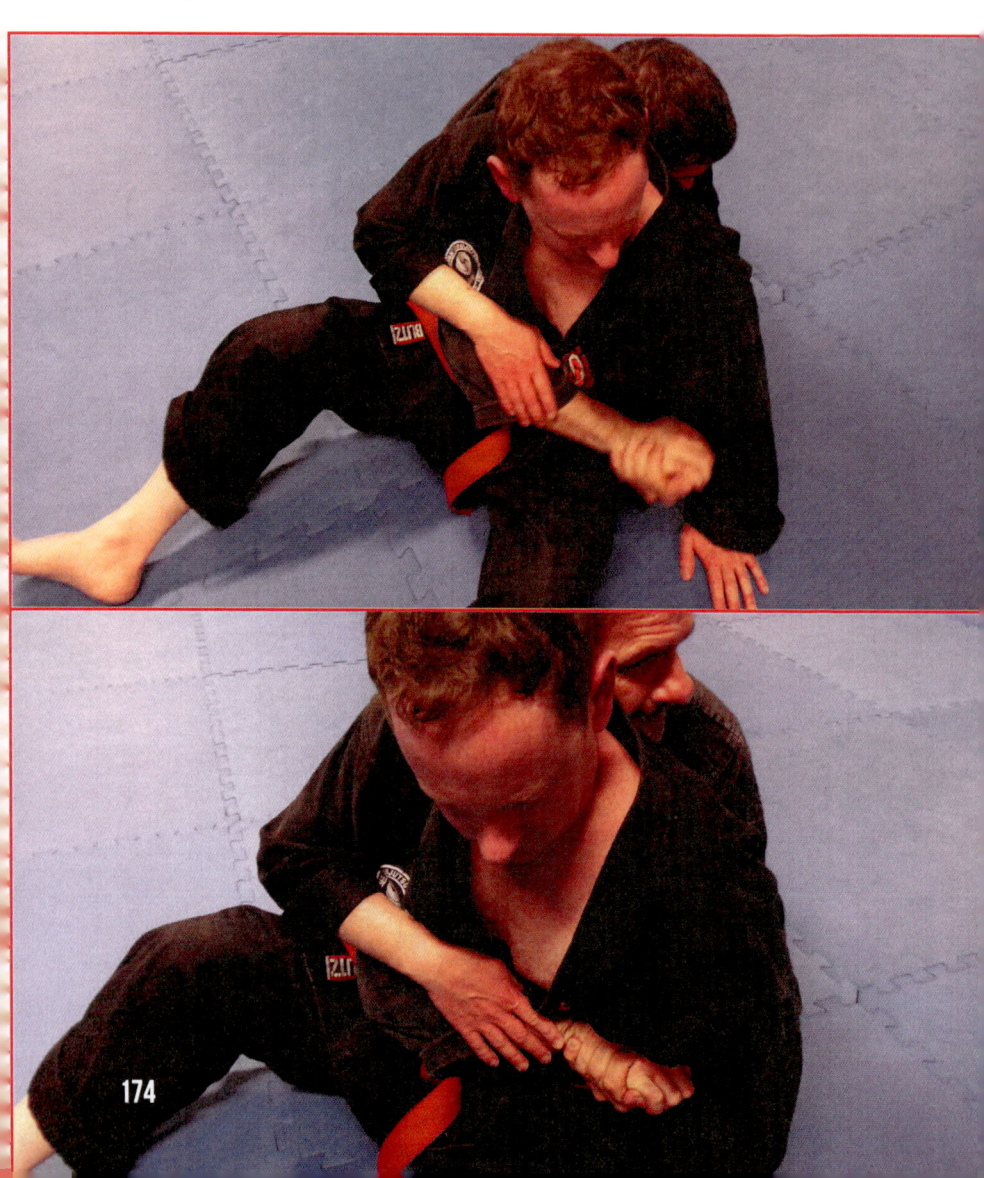

TURNING UKE OVER
FROM ALL FOURS, ONTO THEIR FRONT AND ONTO THEIR BACK.

This exercise helps you learn body mechanics and how to manipulate your opponent. With Uke on all fours (on their hands and knees) try to turn them onto their back. Uke has no or very little resistance to start with, giving Tori plenty of time to practice. You can turn them over and just hold them down or roll them over into a lock or strangle.

Try the same idea but with Uke lying on their front. You will find it easier to turn Uke over as the joints have limited movement. Normally if Uke is on their front it is obviously best to keep them there, as the restricted movement means there's little chance of striking you. But we are just using this as an exercise to learn body mechanics.

With Uke lying on their back you will find it harder to turn them over as the limbs will move around more freely without the chance of getting many locks on that will provide the pain or leverage to turn Uke over. Over the next few pages I have given you some basic ideas to start with but there are many more to practice.

ON ALL FOURS

Grabbing Uke's collar and pulling back. You could also use a strangle, fingers in the eyes, or pull the head back.

Finger under nose. You could also twist the chin or head.

FROM LAYING ON THEIR BACK

Bringing Uke's straight arm across your shin (shin just past the elbow) and pulling Uke around to their front.

Using the elbow or forearm to twist Uke's head.

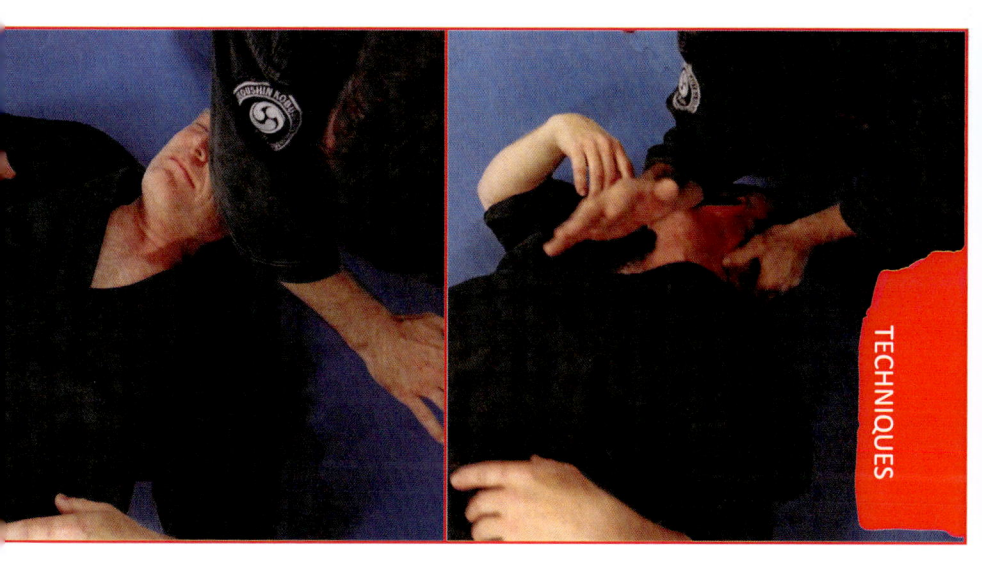

FROM LAYING ON THEIR FRONT

Grabbing under Uke's arm and leg then rolling over.

Rolling Uke over with a lapel strangle.

Turning Uke over by moving a straight arm up to their head and across the back of their shoulders.

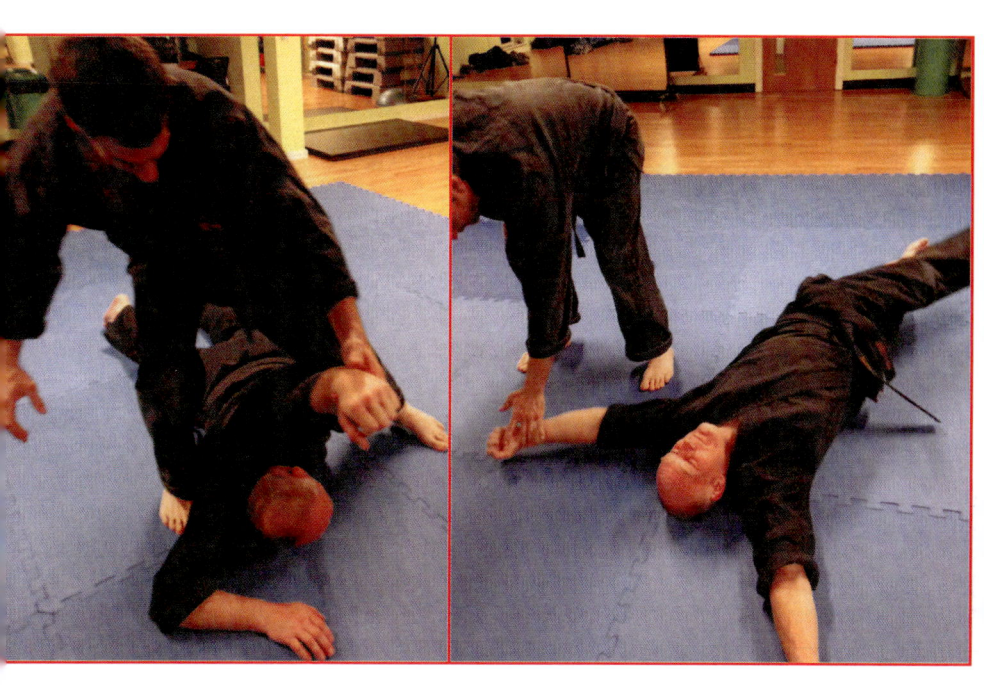

Wrapping Uke's arm around their face, your other hand goes under Uke's closest leg to grab the other leg and pull. This works with Uke on their back or on their front.

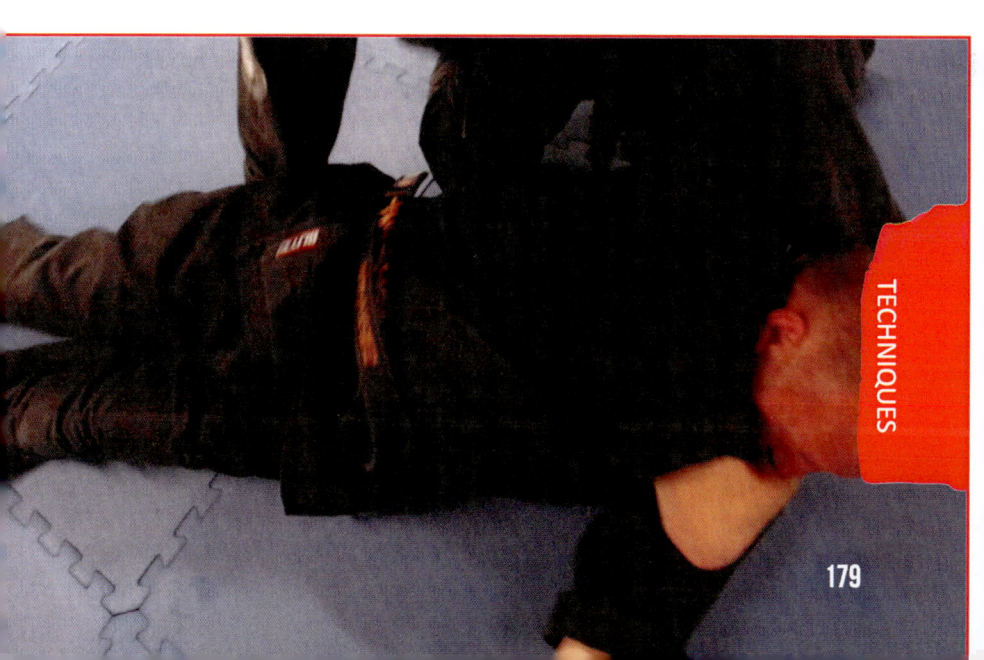

TECHNIQUES

STAYING ON ALL FOURS

Now to turn the tables: you are Uke and on all fours as Tori tries to turn you over and hold you down. Don't have your body too high. Keep your shoulders down for a low centre of gravity. Have your arms and legs just outside of your body and when Tori tries to roll or pull you over extend the arm and leg out to the way you are being tipped. You'll end up feeling like the shovel-snouted lizard on the hot dessert sand. Most of all stay relaxed and don't fight power with power, move your body around to redirect their energy.

PAINFUL DISTRACTION TECHNIQUES

There are some quick distraction techniques to make Uke release a strangle or lock, or to help you turn them where you want them. Grabbing the skin on Uke's lat muscles/sides just under the armpit, grab their skin with your fingers first, then roll your hand into a fist keeping their skin tight as though you are trying to pull it off their body. This is great if Uke is on top of you it makes it easy for you to roll them over.

1. Pinching the inner thigh or inside the upper arm causes instant pain and is fantastic for making Uke release their grip from a strangle or lock.

2. Pulling the top or bottom lip is great for manoeuvring Uke's head ready for a strangle, or to turn them over.

3. Pushing under the nose is useful when Uke is on top and you want to create a bit or room. Lay your finger under their nose and push up.

4. Ippon Ken/single knuckle is the same principle as page 167. Push the knuckle into the back of the jaw, into the temple, through the lip to the top or bottom teeth.

5. Using small joint locks, fingers or toes, basically bend then twist them in the direction they don't want to go.

6. Fingers in the eyes are good for disorientating Uke.

7. Using forearms and elbows across Uke's face or the point of the elbow in the throat, chest or spine, is also effective.

SIT UPS
INCORPORATING REAR NAKED, FIGURE FOUR AND REAR STRANGLE HAND POSITIONS

This little training idea helps you or your students to commit these three techniques to muscle memory whilst also giving the abs a workout and getting a good stretch. Practice both sides. Try to keep your hands close to or touching your legs as much as possible to leave no gaps.

SIT UPS USING THE HADAKA JIME/REAR NAKED CHOKE HAND POSITIONING.

SIT UPS INCORPORATING THE REAR STRANGLE HAND POSITIONING.

SIT UPS INCORPORATING THE FIGURE FOUR HAND POSITIONING

LAST THOUGHTS- FOR NOW

I hope after reading this book you have learnt something to help you or your students. Remember that not everybody bends the same way, has the same flexibility, or has the same pain threshold, so different techniques work better or worse depending on who you are fighting. At the end of the day learn as much as you can because you never know what position you could be in or who you could be fighting against. You must fill your arsenal up to have a better chance to succeed.

I am learning new techniques all the time. Some work and some don't work for me. Some make me think: 'That's so simple – and it works. Fantastic!'. It goes straight in the syllabus. It's worth the effort to keep on training, cross training and going to seminars, events and shows. There is so much more to learn. On the way, you will find that you pick up new favourite techniques and disregard others. Then, many years down the line, you'll see those old techniques again somewhere and it will start you thinking about what you know now, and what you have forgotten.

I've been training for over 36 years now and I'm sure that I have forgotten more techniques than I know now, there is nothing wrong with keeping notes or recording techniques that you have picked up, I always take a note pad with me when going to Seminars or courses and never be afraid to ask questions especially if the technique isn't working as easy as it should, it's normally something simple that needs changing.

ABOUT THE AUTHOR

Simon started his Martial arts adventure in 1980, when he started practicing Judo after 15 years he started to cross train and has practised in many Martial arts over the years from Tai chi to Thai boxing. His love of Martial arts has found him focusing on Karate, Goshin Jutsu and Ju Jutsu. Simon's classes focus very much on being a great all rounder where you are just as at home fighting on the floor as you are fighting standing up and always with no rules (you are fighting for your life not a medal).

Simon currently holds Dan grades in Bujutsu 5th Dan, Goshin Jutsu 5th Dan, Karate 4th Dan and Ju Jutsu 2nd Dan.

Simon regularly teaches and trains at seminars to improve his knowledge in Martial arts and share what he knows with others.

INDEX

Advanced Quick Chokes 165

Arm Crush 54

Armpit Lock 75

Ashi-Dori-Garami 101

Ashi Gake 97, 105-106

Ashi Jime 150

Ashi-Sankaku-Garami 73

Ashi Tori Garami 109

Atama Hishigi 115

Back/Reverse Neck Lock 160

Back Triangle Strangle 142

Back Trunk Strangle 172

Backwards Pulling Neck Lock 164

Belt Strangle 151

Bent-Arm Pin 34

Bent Wrist Lock 91

Bicep Lock 96

Body Cross Hold 22

Breaking The Grip 43

Cross Arm Lock Or Arm Bar 40

Chokes And Strangles 110

Cross-Strangle – Half 134

Cross Strangle – Normal Version 131

Cross-Strangle – Reverse 133

Cross Strangle With Your Back On The Floor 132
Dislocation Of The Knee In 8th Immobilization 108
Double-Hand Choke (Inside) 166
Double-Hand Choke (Outside) 167
Elbow 170
Enpi 170
Entangled Leg Dislocation 101
Entangled Strangle 143
Figure Four, Entangled Lock 61
Finger Choke 168
Foot Choke 150
Foot Entanglement 109
Foot/Heel Hook 106
Foot Lock/Crank 105
Forearm Choke 123
Forearm Strangle 121
From All Fours, Onto Their Front And Onto Their Back. ... 175
From Laying On Their Back 177
From Laying On Their Front 178
Front Naked Choke 157
Front Pulling Neck Lock 162
Front Sliding Collar 124
Front Trunk Strangle 171
Gyaku Juji Jime 133
Gyaku Ude-Garami 69
Hadaka Jime 112
Hadaka Jime 114

Hammer Lock	79
Hand Choke	165
Hand Foot Strangle	137
Hand Trunk Strangle	174
Head/Face Crush	115
Hell Strangle	155
Hiza Gatami	102, 107
Hiza-Hishigi	104
Hiza Ude Gatami	77
Ikkyo	85
Incorporating Rear Naked, Figure Four & Rear Strangle Hand Positions	182
Ippon Ken	169
Jigoku Jime	155
Ju Ji Gatami	40
Kaiten Jime	148
Kata Gatame	24
Kami Shiho Gatame	14
Kata Gatame Jime	145
Kata-Ha-Jime	130
Kata Juji Jime	134
Kata Waza	80
Kesa Gatame	12
Knee Arm Lock	77
Knee Crush/Dislocation	104
Kneeling Shoulder Pin	32
Knee Lock	107

Knife-Hand Strangle	149
Kotegaeshi	84
Kote Guruma Jime	153
Kote Jime	121,123
Kubi Garami	116,158
Last Thoughts- For Now	184
Leg/Foot Locks	97
Loop Choke	153
Lying Back Armpit Lock	78
Mae Do Jime	171
Mae Hadaka Jime	157
Mae Hiki Kubi Gatami	162
Mae Okuri-Eri-Jime	124
Master Lock, Hyper Flexing Wrist Lock	90
Morote Te Jime	166-167
Naked Strangle	114
Nami Juji Jime	131-132
Neck	111
Neck Lock	116, 158
Nejire Kubi Gatami	163
Nikkyo	86
Nippon-Ashi-Hishigi	98
Nodo Hishigi	154
Nukite Jime	168
Obi Jime	151
Okuri-Eri-Jime	129
On All Fours	176

Painful Distraction Techniques 181

Palm Wrist Lock 93

Pin Using Both Shins 36

"Policeman's Pin" 34

Rear Hold... 28

Rear Naked Choke 112

Reverse Figure Four, Reverse Entangled Lock Or Kimura 69

Reverse Scarf Hold 16

Rolling Okuri Eri Jime.. 127

Rolling Strangle 148

Sankuka Jime 138

Sankyo 87

Scarf Hold 12

Sheio-Nage 89

Shime Waza 110

Shotie Gatami 93

Shoulder Hold 24

Shoulder-Hold Strangle 145

Shoulder Lock 80

Shuto Jime 149

Side Four Quarters Hold 18

Side Neck Lock... 159

Side Triangle Strangle 140

Side Trunk Strangle 173

Single Knuckle... 169

Single Leg Crush/Dislocation / Calf Lock............................... 98

Single Wing Choke 130

Sit Ups	182
Sleeve Wheel	122
Sliding Collar Arm Under Uke's	129
Sliding Collar From The Back	125
Sode Guruma Jime	122
Standing Straight-Arm Pin	35
Staying On All Fours	180
Straight-Arm Lock Pin	33
Straight-Knee Lock	102
Tate Shiho Gatame	22
Tate-Shiho-Hiza-Hishigi	108
Te Ashi Jime	137
Tekubi Gatami	90
Te Do Jime	174
Te Jime	165
Throat Crush From Tomoe Nage	154
Thrusting Gi Choke	147
Triangular Entanglement	73
Triangle Strangle	138
Tricep Pin	31
Tsuki Komi Jime	147
Turning Uke Over	175
Turning Wrist Lock	84
Twisitng	42
Twisting Neck Lock	163
Ude Garami	61
Ude Garami Jime	143

Ude Gatami	54
Ude-Hishigi-Waki-Gatame	78
Ura Gatame	28
Ushiro Do Jime	172
Ushiro Hiki Kubi Gatami	164
Ushiro Kesa Gatame	16
Upper Four Quarters Hold	14
Ushiro Kubi Gatami	160
Ushiro Nami Juji Jime	136
Ushiro-Okuri-Eri-Jime	125
Ushiro Sankuka Jime	142
Ushiro Ude Garami	79
Waki Gatami	75
Yoko Do Jime	173
Yoko Kudi Gatami	159
Yoko Sankuka Jime	140
Yoko Shiho Gatame	18
Yonkio	88

NOTES

NOTES

Printed by BoD in Norderstedt, Germany